PENGUIN CLASSICS (P) DELU

THE COLLECTED POEMS

MARCEL PROUST was born on July 10, 1871, in Auteuil, a western section of Paris, where his parents had taken refuge from the constant bombardments of central Paris by advancing and then besieging Prussian armies during the Franco-Prussian War. Just months before his birth, France's Second Empire had fallen, which ushered in the period that is most associated with Proust and his work, the Third Republic. He grew up in Paris, the son of the prominent public health physician Adrien Proust and a well-read Jewish mother, Jeanne (née Weil).

By his late teens, at first through the good offices of his schoolmates at the well-known Lycée Condorcet (where Mallarmé had taught) and then through his own efforts, Proust began to frequent the high society and artistic salons of Paris. In 1896, he published a book of short stories and poems called *Les Plaisirs et les jours* (*Pleasures and Days*). Just after the turn of the century, with the help of his mother and his friend Marie Nordlinger, he published translations of two books by the English critic John Ruskin, though he had little English.

From his experience in society and a lifetime of reading, in 1913 Proust published *Du côté de chez Swann* (rendered in English as *Swann's Way*), which was the first installment of what would become one of the great multivolume novels of the twentieth century, *À la recherche du temps perdu* (called by various translators either *Remembrance of Things Past* or *In Search of Lost Time*). In 1919, the second volume, *À l'ombre des jeunes filles en fleurs* (*In the Shadow of Blooming Young Girls*), won him the prestigious Prix Goncourt. Two more volumes of *À la recherche* were published before Proust died on November 18, 1922—in English, *The Guermantes Way* and *Sodom and Gomorrah*—and the final three—*The Prisoner, Albertine Gone,* and *Time Regained*—after his death.

HAROLD AUGENBRAUM is executive director of the National Book Foundation. Among his books are *Growing Up Latino,*

Encyclopedia Latina, Lengua Fresca, the *Norton Anthology of Latino Literature,* and a translation of Juan Rulfo's *The Plain in Flames* (with Ilan Stavans) and *The Latino Reader* and *U.S. Latino Literature* (with Margarite Fernández-Olmos). His translations for Penguin Classics include Cabeza de Vaca's *Chronicle of the Narváez Expedition* and José Rizal's *Noli Me Tangere* and *El Filibusterismo.* He founded the Proust Society of America in 1996.

TRANSLATORS INCLUDE:

Meena Alexander

Harold Augenbraum

Mary Ann Caws

Nicholas Christopher

Jeff Clark

Lydia Davis

Marcella Durand

Michel Durand

Richard Howard

Wayne Koestenbaum

Charlotte Mandell

Wyatt Mason

Anna Moschovakis

Jennifer Moxley

Ana Oancea

Mark Polizzotti

Susan Stewart

Cole Swensen

Deborah Treisman

Rosanna Warren

Lauren Watel

MARCEL PROUST

The Collected Poems

A DUAL-LANGUAGE EDITION
WITH PARALLEL TEXT

Contributions by
CLAUDE FRANCIS *and* FERNANDE GONTIER

Edited with an Introduction and Notes by
HAROLD AUGENBRAUM

PENGUIN BOOKS

PENGUIN BOOKS
Published by the Penguin Group
Penguin Group (USA) Inc., 375 Hudson Street,
New York, New York 10014, USA

USA | Canada | UK | Ireland | Australia | New Zealand | India | South Africa | China
Penguin Books Ltd, Registered Offices: 80 Strand, London WC2R 0RL, England
For more information about the Penguin Group visit penguin.com

First published in Penguin Books 2013
Poèmes by Marcel Proust, compiled, presented, and annotated by Claude Francis and
Fernande Gontier, published by arrangement with Editions Gallimard, Paris
Copyright © Editions Gallimard, Paris, 1982
Translation copyright © Penguin Group (USA) Inc., 2013
Introduction and notes copyright © Harold Augenbraum, 2013

"Ode à Marcel Proust" from *Poèmes* by Paul Morand. Used by permission of Editions Gallimard, Paris.
Translation from *Modern French Poetry: An Anthology*, edited by Joseph T. Shipley (Greenberg Press, 1926).

Poems 8, 40, 56, 66, 71, 73, 103, and 104, translated by Harold Augenbraum.
Copyright © Harold Augenbram, 2013

Poems 26 and 27 translated by Lydia Davis. Copyright © Lydia Davis, 2013

LIBRARY OF CONGRESS CATALOGING-IN-PUBLICATION DATA
Proust, Marcel, 1871–1922.
Marcel Proust : the collected poems : a dual-language edition with parallel text / compiled by Claude
Francis and Fernande Gontier ; edited with an introduction and notes by Harold Augenbraum.
pages cm
Includes bibliographical references.
ISBN 978-0-14-310690-6
1. Proust, Marcel, 1871–1922—Translations into English.   I. Francis, Claude. II. Gontier, Fernande.
III. Augenbraum, Harold, editor of compilation.   IV. Proust, Marcel, 1871–1922. Poems.
V. Proust, Marcel, 1871–1922. Poems. English.   VI. Title.
PQ2631.R63A2 2013   843'.912—dc23   2012039430

Printed in the United States of America
10 9 8 7 6 5 4 3 2 1
Set in Sabon LT Std
Designed by Spring Hoteling

For Carla and Audri
Vous m'enseignez bien toute une autre douceur

Contents

Introduction

The Novelist's Avocation

> One should always assume that pacts exist between a poet's intelligence and his sensibility, and though he may be unaware of them, he is their plaything.
>
> —Marcel Proust

That Proust wrote poetry comes as a surprise to even avid readers of his work. He is known for his tortured prose, his long sentences, and even his odd behaviors, but in his poems Proust revealed a lesser known side of himself, a personal side that links to his greatest work, but expresses similar themes in a stylistically different way.

The only book by Proust that anyone other than scholars or aficionados reads today is the seven-volume *À la recherche du temps perdu*, or, as its title has been translated into English inadequately, either the mullioned quotation purloined by translator Charles Kenneth Scott Moncrieff (1889–1930) from Shakespeare's Sonnet 30, *Remembrance of Things Past*, or the more recent *In Search of Lost Time*. Proust did publish two other original works in his lifetime, the moony juvenilia *Pleasures and Days*, and a collection of his occasional pieces, *Pastiches et mélanges*.

But his reputation has always hung on the big one. At 1.4

million words it is massive (the word count is approximate: because he never completed it, we have only two or three different postmortem editions to work from, and the literary arguments that take place around them are legion) and it has taken on such a significance in high cultural circles that the author and the book have become synonymous, as happens only with the greats. (Have you read Shakespeare? Have you read Milton? Have you read Proust?) In his case, it only means that one book. Despite the massive biographies, his life has become his work. He is not a historical personage, he is an "it," and his it-ness carries into realms that reach from awe to punch line. The idiosyncrasies of his personal life—especially the cork-lined room—are commonly known to readers throughout the world.

Marcel Proust was born on July 10, 1871, in Auteuil, a western section of Paris that had been annexed to the city in the 1850s by the emperor Napoleon III and his urban planner, Georges-Eugène Haussmann. His father, Adrien Proust, came from Illiers, a small town one hundred miles to the west, scion of a family of Catholic burghers. He had made his name in the successful control of cholera and at the age of thirty-seven married Jeanne Weil, the cultured daughter of affluent Jews with roots in Alsace.

September 1870 was a watershed month in French history. The recurring and anxious line dance of musical chairs among monarch, republic, and empire was coming to an end, though a few grace notes would erupt from time to time, bringing a false sense of change (perhaps these would be better described as a St. Elmo's Fire). On September 2, Napoleon III surrendered himself and his armies after the battle of Sedan, which left the Prussians an open path to the capital. Proust's parents were married on the following day. The day after that, on September 4, the Third Republic was declared. Within months a strangulating siege would take hold of Paris. Regular bombardments of the center city would occur. Communication with the outside world would consist of tying messages to balloons in the hope that they would make it through the phalanx of Prussian sharpshooters.

The populace would be reduced to eating rats. Restaurants—according to observers—began to serve the cooked flesh of zoo animals.

That winter, as Jeanne's pregnancy progressed, to escape the upheaval of the center city the Prousts retreated to Jeanne's uncle Louis Weil's house in Auteuil. Dr. Proust continued to commute to see his patients in the center, and barely escaped gunshots at least once. There has long been speculation that such anxiety produced Proust's nervous disposition. He was baptized a Catholic in the église Saint-Louis-d'Antin and spent spring and some summer vacations at the home of his father's family in Illiers, which, because he helped fictionalize it in his book, later took on the patina of Proust's fictional town, which is now legally called Illiers-Combray. A sign in a local storefront window says, "The bakery where Aunt Léonie bought her madeleines." The town where his father grew up is now only partly real, and Proust the author is a literary tourist site.

Proust was nine years old and playing in the park of the Champs-Elysées when he had his first asthma attack. For the rest of his life—to breathe, to sleep—he would medicate himself: Trional, Legras fumigations in the closed room of his apartment, Espic's cigarettes . . . and more and more coffee. The asthma, the years he spent in the Lycée Condorcet, where he would meet many of his upper-class and aristocratic friends, and, above all, reading, reading, and more reading would engrave themselves on his view of personal well-being, French society, and the centrality of art to the ongoing reinvention of humanness.

By adolescence he had transformed himself from the scion of a seriously engaged family into society's perception of a flatterer and a fop. His parents worried about his lack of will. His guilt over their anxiety would increase manyfold because at that time French men lived in their parents' homes until they married. He would transfer a complex guilt into À la recherche. It would intensify after his father's death in 1903 and especially his mother's in 1905. At the age of twenty-five, he had published Les Plaisirs et les jours (Pleasures and Days), a collection of poetry and short prose, and, later, translations of two books by his then-hero, the British critic John Ruskin. But an ill feeling stemming from a lack of achievement gnawed at him until, after two abortive attempts—studies by the artist as a young man which were later published as *Jean Santeuil* and *Contre Sainte-Beuve*—between 1907 and 1909 he found not his vocation—he had always known that—but his voice. His notebook of 1908 began with chaotic jottings, but it progressed in fits and starts until it became the scrim of *À la recherche du temps perdu*. Characters emerged, situations evolved. With each notebook tangentials receded until outside glosses are unnecessary for even the general Proust reader. Therein the Proustian world comes into focus, becomes recognizable, and its writer becomes Proust, the guy we know, *our* Proust. Over his shoulder was the ending of the final impersonation of monarchy lifted away by uncertainty, hubris, and incompetence, its denizens hanging on to a vision of hierarchy the way scales will cling to one's eyes. In front of him was a neverending phantasma, a series of planned and unplanned writing sessions, deteriorating health, withdrawal, and obsession with his work. His was the feverish subscription of the past before the inevitability of a foreshortened future. He scribbled, he scrawled, he threw scraps of paper onto the floor for his housekeeper to collect and transcribe. He pasted narrow sheets on top of manuscript, typescript, and typeset pages—the famous "papyroles"—frantically "dilating" his prose, as Richard Howard has described it, pushing the boundaries of his own work again and again and again until he died. His was not a race against time or a race with death. It was more of a transcription of the longevity of his vital energies, a reformatting of duration by limitless, imaginative work.

He translated his social experience into a pestiferous Vanity Fair; through artistry he blended many blatherings into the coherence of art. It was the age of monocles, of a trite and precipitous class of heraldic leftovers pretending in their dramatic way that democracy was irrelevant, that society was mere theater, and prurience was simply a way of life; men and, later, women whose captive sense of the gimlet eye traded itself for pretension and affectation and made the class into which Proust exchanged worldly for societal ambition an object lesson in puffery, his own and that of others. While as time passed his participation in "society" faded—but never disappeared—into hermitage and obsession, theirs continued a daily pattern of misrecognition. Proust's friend Louis de Robert wrote that "Proust was truly fortunate that his illnesses had him captive in bed for fifteen years, in a closed room and thus afforded him the leisure to write *À la recherche du temps perdu*. Without that, what would he have been? A charming being, a cultivated mind, a brilliant conversationalist, in sum, a man who leaves not a trace."

But you don't learn lessons from Proust's life and work, as Alain de Botton has whimsically written. Instead you observe the delicacy with which he places words and phrases beside one another, building and unbuilding momentum until insight itself dilates and elongates. His style put some readers off. Paul Bourget loathed it, René Boylesve admired it (the two appear together in Poem 42). By the time he died, in November 1922, the year in which James Joyce's *Ulysses* was published in Paris and Eliot's *The Waste Land* in London, he was a famous writer, though it would take the Americans and the Germans to convince the French that such fame was warranted.

After Proust began the composition of *In Search of Lost Time*, writing poetry was akin to taking a busman's holiday from literature, like an undertaker who visits the local wax museum on his day off. His favorites continued to be Baudelaire, whom he would mimic, praise, and challenge at various stages of his life, Gérard de Nerval, Leconte de Lisle, Paul Verlaine, and sometimes even Stéphane Mallarmé, of the local generation, who had taught at the Lycée Condorcet where Proust was a day boy, though the two would feud in print over "obscurity" in the poetry of the symbolists.

Even in the poems, especially the later ones, he appears to be an odd duck—stranger still after his parents' deaths—and he slowly withdrew from social life to concentrate on his Big Book,

his legacy. Contemporary memoirs and letters catalogue his id-
iosyncrasies, his weirdly, almost untethered appearance late in
his life. Marthe Bibesco barely contains her contempt, Laure de
Chevigné and Winnie Singer their exasperation. An American
wrote that he had never seen a man eat dinner while wearing his
overcoat. Several friends noted that Proust's cotton bunting, a
stuffing against the cold even on hot days, often peeked out from
beneath his collar.

But if the Big Book is the culmination of observing and ab-
sorbing social surroundings and art, and if one's aesthetic is
composed of what one puts in and what one leaves out—that
Janus-like entourage of competing problematics—then Proust
signals his intentions for his great work of fiction in his letters
and verse. The collected letters are like a vast army, hundreds of
them creating a series of brigades in the twenty-one volumes
compiled by the Proustmaster Philip Kolb. An early analyst,
Pierre Raphael, likened them to *À la recherche*: "The correspon-
dence doesn't diverge from *Lost Time*. In the novel and in the
letters, we find the same thinking."

So what space do the poems occupy in the Proustian land-
scape? When *Swann's Way* was published in 1913, Proust en-
tered the narrow corridor of literary fame. With each subsequent
publication, even he recognized that his life and work would
become a diorama. After noting the revelations contained in the
published correspondence of other writers, he consulted his
business and legal brain trust—bankers Horace Finaly and Li-
onel Hauser—about securing his own letters from publication
after his death. They told him it would be impossible to do so.
It's hard to imagine that he expected the poems would be tracked
down and collected. They were occasional pieces to friends.
Some he asked to be destroyed. Most likely he didn't even re-
member having written others since they were dashed off on
scraps of paper and envelopes. The poems are harmonic elabora-
tions on the symphony of *In Search of Lost Time*, the principal
motif of Proust's life and career.

One of the things that makes reading Proust's poems so enjoy-
able is that he removed them from the water gates of early mod-

ernism, leaving them instead in the late Romantic, early modern period of Baudelaire and Nerval, giving them a human—as opposed to a consciously artificed—aspect. They lean into traditional form as if Proust were putting a shoulder to a buttress. In reading them, one also has to recant the expectation of the brain-teasing, tongue-twisting, language-torturing sentences of the Big Book and reimagine Our Proust as a personable human being, a fun guy who liked to josh with his friends, the party-goer who was known as a superb mimic, Louis de Robert's "brilliant conversationalist," and a jokester, the youngster who tried to pick up the dairy barmaid on the way home from the Lycée Condorcet, who serenaded Jeanne Pouquet with a tennis racket, who exchanged baby-talk letters with his best friend Reynaldo Hahn. Like a series of papyroles pasted onto a biography, one reads them to get insight into the writer's development more as person than writer.

They show a different side of Proust from the Great Writer to whom we have become accustomed and inured: at various times intimate, vulgar, gay, Proust as Wicked Little Imp, master of the affectionate barb. Knowing this Proust only enhances our appreciation of the novel. As you read the poems, the lapidary wall of Great Writer dissolves and the person expands horizontally, while at the same time the importance of friendship draws out a consistent beauty of form and language, full of sentiment without sentimentality:

> My friendship for you, so delicate and true
> Has killed for all time any feeling I had for her
> If ever it had been born in my heart
> Where you possess, my dear friend, the best part.

Or vulgar snickering about friends:

> They say a Russian, may God preserve his soul,
> Managed to rouse a flutter of sensation
> In Ferdinand's leathery, tanned, and well-worked hole
> By slipping in up to the hilt his brave baton.

The poems were composed from when Proust was seventeen to when he was fifty. The early ones show his interest in the interplay of the arts, which he never deserts and which he carries through *Jean Santeuil* and *Contre Sainte-Beuve* into *À la recherche*, in the integration of genres and disciplines in the "Portraits de peintres" and "Portraits de musiciens." They cover the yearnings of juvenilia, sexual longing laced with the flippancy of narcissism. They continue with poems of homage, imitations and intimations of other famous poets composed with forethought and almost foreordained. The very bookish Marcel Proust was above all a reader, a logophile who imbibed literature to such an extent that one imagines by the time he reached adulthood he no longer knew where the memory of Baudelaire's work ended and the vision of his own poetry began. Tone wells up from the deeply digested work of precursors.

The later ones nip, bite, and jab at the social circles that figure so prominently in *À la recherche*. His pastiches juggle creativity and criticism, an inside-out analysis of those precursors' work, which looked nothing like the analysis he would venture in his articles and essays because in them he can be camp, a word we can only use in retrospect. By the time he was writing his novel, had found his vocation and his voice, he could also relieve the burdens of that voice by engaging in the avocation of poetry. Perhaps, in the end, his true poetic voice is represented by the late, personal poems: playful and "wicked," in the late twentieth-century meaning of that word, comic and arch, at once charming and charged, devoid of the embedded pathos that characterizes even the most comically serious satire of the *Recherche*. If, as Louis de Robert notes, Proust's letters have the verve of the best pages of *À la recherche du temps perdu*, his later poems reflect more the daily Proust, the playful Proust, the ludic Proust of nom de plume newspaper reports and pastiches.

In the end, these poems, gathered together—which they were never intended to be—form an intimate portrait of a great writer of huge reputation, different from the image one derives from the fiction and the letters. They may cover the same ground as the *Search*, but unlike the Big Book they were not rewritten many times, and they represent a shortening of the distance between creator and reader, not a lengthening. At various times they are sexed-up, dreamy, artsy, catty, and loving. They are always observant, insightful, and delightful.

Suggestions for Further Reading

Works by Proust

Proust, Marcel. *À la recherche du temps perdu*. Paris: Bibliothèque de la Pléaide, 1987–1989. Four volumes with notes and drafts.

————. *Carnets*. Edited by Florence Callu and Antoine Compagnon. Paris: Gallimard, 2002.

————. *Contre Sainte-Beuve, suivi de nouveaux mélanges*. Edited by Bernard de Fallois. Paris: Gallimard, 1954.

————. *Correspondance*, volumes 1–21, edited by Philip Kolb. Paris: Plon, 1970–1993.

————. *Écrits de jeunesse 1887–1895*. Illiers-Combray: Institut Marcel Proust International, 1991.

————. *Essais et articles*. Edited by Thierry Laget. Paris: Gallimard, 1994.

————. *Jean Santeuil*. Edited by Bernard de Fallois. Paris: Gallimard, 1954.

————. *Les Plaisirs et les jours*. Paris: Calmann-Levy, 1896.

————. *Pastiches et mélanges*. Paris: Éditions de la Nouvelle revue française, 1919.

————. *Poèmes*. Edited by Claude Francis and Fernande Gontier. Cahiers Marcel Proust, no. 10. Paris: Gallimard, 1982.

Works About Proust and His Times

Astruc, Gabriel. *Le Pavillon des fantômes: Mémoires*. Paris: Bernard Grasset, 1929.

Bac, Ferdinand (Ferdinand Sigismund Bach). *Intimités de la IIIème Ré-*

publique: Tome 2: La Fin des 'temps delicieux': Souvenirs parisiens. Paris: Hachette, 1935.

Battersea, Constance de R. F. *Reminiscences*. London: Macmillan and Company, 1923.

Benda, Julien. *La Jeunesse d'un clerc*. Paris: Gallimard, 1936.

———. *Un regulier dans le siècle*. Paris: Gallimard, 1938.

Bertho, Sophie, ed. *Proust et ses peintres*. Amsterdam–Atlanta: Éditions Rodopi, 2000.

Bibesco, Marthe. *Au Bal avec Marcel Proust*. Paris: Gallimard, 1928.

———. *Pourquoi j'écris? De peur d'oublier la vie: Ainsi parla . . . la Princesse Bibesco*. Paris: Éditions Nilsson, 1930.

———. *Proust's Oriane: A Diptych* (translation by Edward Marsh of *La duchesse de Guermantes*). London: Falcon Press, 1952.

———. *Le Voyageur voilé*. Paris: La Palatine, 1949. Available in English as *The Veiled Wanderer*.

Billy, Robert de. *Marcel Proust: Lettres et conversations*. Paris: Éditions des Portiques, 1930.

Blanche, Jacques-Emile. *La Pêche aux souvenirs*. Paris: Flammarion, 1949.

———. *Mes Modèles*. Paris: Stock, 1929.

Bloch-Dano, Evelyne. *Madame Proust*, translated by Alice Kaplan. Chicago: University of Chicago Press, 2007.

Bourget, Paul. *Gladys Harvey*. Paris, 1888.

Cambor, Kate. *Gilded Youth: Three Lives in France's Belle Epoque*. New York: Farrar, Straus & Giroux, 2009.

Carter, William C. *Marcel Proust: A Life*. New Haven, CT: Yale University Press, 2000.

———, editor. *The UAB Marcel Proust Symposium*. Birmingham, AL: Summa Publications, 1989.

Castellane, Boniface de. *Comment j'ai decouvert l'Amérique*. Paris: Les Éditions G. C. Crès, 1924.

———. *L'Art d'être pauvre: Mémoires*. Paris: Les Éditions G. C. Crès, 1925.

Claudel, Paul. *Contacts et circonstances*. Paris: Gallimard, 1940.

Clermont-Tonnerre, Elisabeth de. *Robert de Montesquiou et Marcel Proust*. Paris: Flammarion, 1925.

Compagnon, Antoine. *Proust entre deux siècles*. Paris: Éditions du Seuil, 1989.

————, editor. *Proust, la mémoire et la littérature*. Paris: Odile Jacob, 2009.

Cossart, Michael de. *The Food of Love: Princesse Edmond de Polignac (1865–1943) and Her Salon*. London: Hamish Hamilton, 1978.

Curtiss, Mina. *Bizet and His World*. New York: Vienna House, 1974.

————. *Other People's Letters*. Boston: Houghton Mifflin, 1978.

Daudet, Julia. *Souvenirs autour d'un groupe littéraire*. Paris: E. Fasquelle, 1910.

Daudet, Léon. *Salons et journaux*. Paris: Bernard Grasset, 1932.

Davenport-Hines, Richard. *Proust at the Majestic: The Last Days of the Author Whose Book Changed Paris*. New York: Bloomsbury USA, 2006.

Descaves, Pierre. *Mes Goncourt*. Paris: Robert Laffont, 1949.

Diesbach, Ghislain de. *La Princesse Marthe Bibesco, 1886–1973*. Paris: Perrin, 1986.

Dolamore, Susan M. *French Autobiographical Writing, 1900–1950*. London: Grant & Cutler, 1997.

Dreyfus, Robert. *Souvenirs sur Marcel Proust*. Paris: Bernard Grasset, 1926.

Fargue, Leon-Paul. *Refuges*. Paris: Émile-Paul Frères, 1942.

Ferré, André. *Les Années de collège de Marcel Proust*. Paris: Gallimard, 1959.

Flament, Albert. *Le Bal du Pré-Catelan*. Paris: Fayard, 1946.

Fouquières, André de. *Mon Paris et ses Parisiens*. Paris: Horay, 1953.

Gavoty, Bernard. *Reynaldo Hahn: Le musicien de la Belle Epoque*. Paris: Éditions Buchet/Chastel, 1976.

Germain, André. *Les Fous de 1900*. Paris: La Palatine, 1954.

————. *La Bourgeoisie qui brûle*. Paris: Sun, 1951.

Gramont, Elisabeth de. *Marcel Proust*. Paris: Flammarion, 1948.

————. *Souvenirs du monde de 1890 à 1940*. Paris: Bernard Grasset, 1966.

Gregh, Fernand. *L'Age d'or: souvenirs d'enfance et de jeunesse*. Paris: Bernard Grasset, 1947.

————. *L'Age d'airain*. Paris: Bernard Grasset, 1951.

————. *Mon amitié avec Marcel Proust: Souvenirs et lettres inédites*. Paris: Bernard Grasset, 1958.

Griffin, Susan. *The Book of the Courtesans*. New York: Broadway Books, 2001.

Halévy, Daniel. *Pays Parisiens*. Paris: Éditions Émile-Paul Frères, 1929.

Huddleston, Sisley. *Paris Salons, Cafes, Studios*. New York: J. B. Lippincott, 1928.

Jullian, Philippe. *Prince of Aesthetes: Count Robert de Montesquiou, 1855–1921*. New York: Viking Press, 1978.

Lauris, Georges de. *À un ami: Correspondance inedite de Marcel Proust, 1903–1922*. Paris: Amiot-Dumont, 1948.

———. *Souvenirs d'une belle époque*. Paris: Amiot-Dumont, 1948.

Lesage, Laurent. *Marcel Proust and His Literary Friends*. Urbana: University of Illinois Press, 1958.

Martin-Fugier, Anne. *Les Salons de la IIIe République: Art, littérature, politique*. Paris: Perrin, 2009.

Maurois, André. *À la recherche de Marcel Proust*. Paris: Hachette, 1949.

Mein, Margaret. *A Foretaste of Proust: A Study of Proust and His Precursors*. Farnborough, UK: Saxon House, 1974.

Montesquiou-Fésenzac, Robert de. *Les pas effacés*. Paris: Émile-Paul Frères, 1923.

Morand, Paul. *Tendres Stocks*. Paris: Gallimard, 1921.

———. *1900*. Paris: Les Éditions de France, 1931.

———. *Le visiteur du soir*. Genève: La Palatine, 1949.

Muhlstein, Anka. *Monsieur Proust's Library*. New York: Other Press, 2012.

Noailles, Anna de. *Le Livre de ma vie*. Paris: Hachette, 1932.

Pouquet, Jeanne-Maurice. *Le Salon de Madame Arman de Caillavet*. Paris: Hachette, 1926.

———. *Quelques lettres de Marcel Proust à Jeanne, Simone, et Gaston de Caillavet, Robert de Flers, et Bertrand de Fénelon*. Paris: Hachette, 1929.

Prestwich, P. F. *The Translation of Memories: Recollections of the Young Proust from the Letters of Marie Nordlinger*. London: Peter Owen, 1999.

Riquetti de Mirabeau, Sibylle-Gabrielle-Marie-Antoinette de, *La Joyeuse enfance de la IIIe République*. Paris: Calmann-Levy, 1931.

Rivière, Jacques, editor. *Cahier Marcel Proust, numéro 1: Hommage à Marcel Proust.* Paris: Gallimard, 1927.

Robert, Louis de. *De l'Amour à la Sagesse.* Paris: Eugene Figuiere, Editeur, 1930.

———. *De Loti à Proust: Souvenirs et confidences.* Paris: E. Flammarion, 1928.

Robitaille, Martin. *Proust épistolier.* Montréal: Presses de l'Université de Montréal, 2003.

Rosengarten, Frank. *The Writings of the Young Marcel Proust (1885–1900): An Ideological Critique.* New York: Peter Lang, 2001.

Rosny, J-H. *Mémoires de la vie littéraire.* Paris: G. Cres, 1922.

———. *Portraits et souvenirs.* Paris: Compagnie française des arts graphiques, 1945.

Rostand, Maurice. *Confession d'un demi-siècle.* Paris: La Jeune Parque, 1948.

Scaraffia, Giuseppe. *Marcel Proust.* Pordenone: Edizione Studio Tesi, 1986.

Scheikévitch, Marie. *Time Past.* Boston: Houghton Mifflin, 1935.

Schlumberger, Jean. *Eveils.* Paris: Gallimard, 1950.

Silvera, Alain. *Daniel Halévy and His Times.* Ithaca, NY: Cornell University Press, 1966.

Stavinsky, Igor. *Chroniques de ma vie.* Paris: Éditions Denoel et Steele, 1935.

Strauss, Walter A. *Proust and Literature: The Novelist as Critic.* Cambridge, MA: Harvard University Press, 1957.

Sutherland, Christine. *Enchantress: Marthe Bibesco and Her World.* New York: Farrar, Straus & Giroux, 1996.

Tadié, Jean-Yves. *Marcel Proust: A Life.* Translated by Euan Cameron. New York: Viking Press, 2000.

———, editor. *Proust et ses amis.* Paris: Gallimard, 2010. An edition of the *Cahier Marcel Proust.*

Vassili, Paul. *France from Behind the Veil: Fifty Years of Social and Political Life.* London: Cassell and Company, 1914.

Wharton, Edith. *A Backward Glance.* New York and London: D. Appleton–Century, 1934.

A Note on the Text

The Collected Poems of Marcel Proust was based for the most part on the extraordinary literary detective work of Claude Francis and Fernande Gontier, the results of which were published as *Poèmes* in the *Cahiers Marcel Proust* in 1982, with additional discoveries by Anne Borrel and others.

With the few exceptions of the early poems that were not included in that publication, the order follows that of Francis and Gontier, which divides them into early works, which were generally composed before Proust was twenty-five; burlesques and satires; and poems dedicated to individuals. For poems that were published during Proust's lifetime, when it can be ascertained or approximated a publication date has been included in the endnotes. Dating those that were not published during Proust's lifetime (and few were) is often problematic. Many were enclosed in personal letters—or were the entire communication—but Proust rarely dated his letters. The general correspondence, however, which included all of Proust's letters that had come to light through the 1970s, was edited by Philip Kolb, who with remarkable research and aplomb was able to create an epistolary chronology through the use of cultural "vectors" using information culled from publications of the time and letters of Proust's friends and acquaintances. When Proust included a title, it has been included here. I have placed the notes at the back of the book in order to allow the poetry to stand alone. The notes do not include what in French are called *variantes*. These possible "variations" are inevitable since unpublished poems do not benefit from a "final" version. For readers who are interested in seeing these variations, visit the *Cahier* noted above.

I have seen only one other translation of these poems into another language: Franco Fortini's 1989 publication in Italian, published by Einaudi. Fortini omitted Poem 27 because it "seemed to be a translation from Heine"; four early poems discovered by Anne Borrel and published in *Écrits de jeunesse* in 1991 (numbers 1, 2, 4 and 6 in this collection); and poems 103 and 104, which were found in other sources. Fortini also transformed the poems into an odd hybrid of poetry and prose, with no line breaks.

In developing these original translations, it was felt that the best way to express Proust's poetry was to ask poets to translate them into verse. The approach to each poem was left up to the individual, including whether or not to follow Proust's rhyme scheme. Proust's prose from *Les Plaisirs et les jours* has been translated into English at least twice, but in both instances the poetry was omitted, so all translations herein are appearing in book form for the first time. I would like to thank the twenty extraordinary translators who brought them from Proust's mauve light to their own. For their many kinds of help, I would also like to thank the staff at The New York Public Library, Gallimard's Anne-Solange Noble, Penguin's Elda Rotor and Henry Freedland, Bill Carter, Michael Millman, Alice Kaplan, Fiona and Stan Burnett, Burton Pike, Rose Vekony, Meriam Korichi, and my fellow members of the Proust Society, with loving memory of Esther Kraman. Finally, special thanks to my sister, Marjorie Augenbraum, for her insights into the world of the visual arts in this period.

The Collected Poems

LES INTERMITTENCES
DU CŒUR

THE INTERMITTENCES OF
THE HEART

I

PÉDÉRASTIE

À Daniel Halévy

Si j'avais un gros sac d'argent d'or ou de cuivre
Avec un peu de nerf aux reins lèvres ou mains
Laissant ma vanité—cheval, sénat ou livre,
Je m'enfuirais là-bas, hier, ce soir ou demain

Au gazon framboisé—émeraude ou carmin !—
Sans rustiques ennuis, guêpes, rosée ou givre
Je voudrais à jamais coucher, aimer ou vivre
Avec un tiède enfant, Jacques, Pierre ou Firmin.

Arrière le mépris timide des Prud'hommes !
Pigeons, neigez ! Chantez, ormeaux ! blondissez, pommes !
Je veux jusqu'à mourir aspirer son parfum !

Sous l'or des soleils roux, sous la nacre des lunes
Je veux . . . m'évanouir et me croire défunt
Loin du funèbre glas des Vertus importunes !

PEDERASTY

To Daniel Halévy

If I had money from a boundless mint
and sinew enough in hands, lips, loins,
I'd shun the vanity of politics and print,
and leave—tomorrow? No, *tonight*!—for lawns

luminous with artificial green
(*without* the rustic flaws of frost and vermin),
where I'd forever be sleeping with one
warm child or other: François? Firmin? . . .

For what is *manly mockery* to me?
Let Sodom's apples burn, acre by acre,
I'd savor still the sweat of those sweet limbs!

Beneath a solar gold, a lunar nacre,
I'd . . . *languish* (an *ars moriendi* of my own),
deaf to the knell of dreary Decency!

VERS À LAURE HAYMAN

Sous l'ombre où le lilas s'éplore
Consolé de furtif soleil
Près d'un ruisseau qu'un halo laure
    Voici Laure !

Reine à la chevelure de soleil
La splendeur des astres te dore
Et les perles de Baltimore
Et ton sang aux couchants pareils
    Laure !

Col grêle ainsi qu'un pilastre maure
Seins clairs qu'une rose honore
Éclose en sa neige, au soleil
Discours fastueux et vermeil
    De Laure !

Certes l'Éros qui te colore
Est un chasseur non-pareil
Qui dans ce monde de sommeil
Nous poursuit. Je serai mort au réveil.

Mon esprit glorieux ne verra point l'aurore
Mais un dieu t'envoya ; tueuse, je t'adore !
Je t'ai tressé ce diadème : qu'il te laure,
    Laure !

LINES TO LAURE HAYMAN

In the shade where lilacs weep
Consoled by a sun that slips
Along a stream the laurels adorn
    Behold Laure!

Queen with the sun in her hair
Gilded by the splendor of stars
As by your Baltimore pearls
And your sunset blood all the more
    Laure!

Neck smooth as the marble of Moors
Breasts pale as blessed by a rose
In full sun as it opens its snow
The lavish, dusky lore
    Of Laure!

Of course, Eros who gives you your note
Is a hunter whose equal's unknown
Who tracks us down through the world of pre-dawn.
I'll be dead when I awake

So shall not see the day that breaks
Upon the God who sent you forth, Fatale whom I adore!
I wove you this crown, these laurels for
    Laure!

3

Sonnet en pensant à Daniel Halévy pendant qu'on marque les absents

Ses yeux sont comme les noires nuits brillantes ;
C'est la tête fine des forts égyptiens
Qui dressent leurs poses lentes
Sur les sarcophages anciens.

Son nez est fort et délicat
Comme les clairs chapiteaux grêles ;
Ses lèvres ont le sombre éclat
Des rougissantes airelles.

Sur sa riche âme, rieuse en sa sauvagerie,
L'univers se reflète ainsi
Qu'une glorieuse imagerie

Cependant qu'un feu subtil et choisi
Anime cette âme et ce corps nubique
D'une exquise vivacité féerique.

3

SONNET THINKING OF DANIEL HALÉVY WHILE NOTI THOSE WHO ARE ABSENT

His eyes are like black bejeweled nights;
His refined head that of strong Egyptians
Who lift their slow poses
On ancient sarcophagi.

His nose is strong and delicate
like clear, slender capitals;
His lips have the somber splendor
Of ripening berries.

Upon his ample soul, laughing in its savagery,
The universe is reflected, as well
As a glorious imagery

Meanwhile, a subtle, select fire
Quickens that soul and that nubile physique
With a liveliness, exquisite and magic.

4

À Daniel Halévy

En le regardant, pendant le premier quart d'heure de colle.

Tamisé, le soleil égoutte ses pleurs d'or
Sous la paix du sapin vénérable qui dort
Tamisé, le soleil sème des taches blanches
Aux pieds des vieux sapins violés de pervenches.

Tamisé le soleil attiédit ses opales
Sur la fraîcheur des lacs nimbés de brouillards pâles

Rêve morbide ! . . . Ô Roi cruel, jeune Tueur
Père accablant du lourd sommeil de la sueur.

Depuis l'Éternité du Rêve tu tourmentes
Les hommes musculeux, les vierges charmantes
Et tu mets l'aiguillon du Mal dans leur néant
Tu lasses de lumière Ô Roi très accablant
Et je sens m'irriter lentes et douloureuses
Des splendeurs de soleil et des paresses d'yeuses
Dormant à l'ombre au lourd soleil, en plein midi.

Puisque je suis rivé par le Rêve mauvais
A ton exécrable Palais.
Pour la vie Ô Soleil. Du moins je te maudis
Et je veux chaque jour saigner ton sang, ta mort
Je te maudis au nom des pâles noctambules

4

To Daniel Halévy

While Looking at Him During the First Quarter of an Hour of Detention.

Sifted, the sun drips its gold tears
Beneath a peaceful, sleeping pine
Sifted, the sun sows its white drops
At the feet of old pines violated by periwinkle.

Sifted, the sun chills its opals
On cool lakes wreathed by pale mist

Morbid dream! . . . O cruel king, young killer,
Overwhelming sire of the heavy sleep of sweat.

From the eternity of dream you torment
Muscular men and charming virgins
And their nothingness you pierce with evil
O oppressive King you weary of light
And sleeping in the shade of heavy noon sun
I feel the slow and painful irritation
Of sun splendors and sluggish oaks

Because I'm riveted to your execrable palace
by an evil dream.
O sun for life. At the very least I curse you
And every day I want to bleed your blood, your death
I curse you in the name of pale night owls

Des assoiffés de métalliques crépuscules
Qui déçus dans leur rêve héroïque et troublant
Te maudissent Ô Roi cruel farouche et blanc
Et songent aux fraîcheurs bleuissantes des nuits
Près des mystique chats . . .

Of those who thirst in metallic dusk
Disillusioned in heroic and disturbing dreams
Who curse you, O cruel, fierce, white King
And think of the bluish coolness of nights
Near mystical cats . . .

5

JE CONTEMPLE SOUVENT LE CIEL DE MA MÉMOIRE

Le temps efface tout comme effacent les vagues
Les travaux des enfants sur le sable aplani
Nous oublierons ces mots si précis et si vagues
Derrière qui chacun nous sentions l'infini.

Le temps efface tout il n'éteint pas les yeux
Qu'ils soient d'opale ou d'étoile ou d'eau claire
Beaux comme dans le ciel ou chez un lapidaire
Ils brûleront pour nous d'un feu triste ou joyeux.

Les uns joyaux volés de leur écrin vivant
Jetteront dans mon cœur leurs durs reflets de pierre
Comme au jour où sertis, scellés dans la paupière
Ils luisaient d'un éclat précieux et décevant.

D'autres doux feux ravis encor par Prométhée
Étincelle d'amour qui brillait dans leurs yeux
Pour notre cher tourment nous l'avons emportée
Clartés trop pures ou bijoux trop précieux.

Constellez à jamais le ciel de ma mémoire
Inextinguibles yeux de celles que j'aimai
Rêvez comme des morts, luisez comme des gloires
Mon cœur sera brillant comme une nuit de Mai.

L'oubli comme une brume efface les visages
Les gestes adorés au divin autrefois,
Par qui nous fûmes fous, par qui nous fûmes sages
Charmes d'égarement et symboles de foi.

I OFTEN CONTEMPLATE
MY MEMORY'S SKIES

Time erases all just as the waves
Efface the children's castles on the beach
We'll forget these words so precise, so vague
Still sensing the infinite behind each.

Time effaces all it does not erase the eyes
Be they of star, clear water, or opal
As rich in the skies or on the jeweler's table
They flame for us, joyous or sadly wise.

The joyous, flown from their living bevels,
Will pierce my heart with their gem-hard glints
As on the day they were set in their lids
Gleaming with a precious, deceptive sparkle.

Other sweet fires Prometheus ravished
Have sparked a love that flashes in their eyes
With a brilliance too pure and jewels too lavish
We carry it off in a torrent of sighs.

Constellate ever my memory's skies
Dream like the dead and gleam like the day
To all whom I loved for your endless eyes
My heart will shine like a night in May.

Forgetting, like a mist, erases faces
Adoring gestures to gods now dead
Who drove us wise, who drove us mad
The errant spells and faithful traces.

Le temps efface tout l'intimité des soirs
Mes deux mains dans son cou vierge come la neige
Ses regards caressants mes nerfs comme un arpège
Le printemps secouant sur nous ses encensoirs.

D'autres, les yeux pourtant d'une joyeuse femme,
Ainsi que des chagrins étaient vastes et noirs
Épouvante des nuits et mystère des soirs
Entre ces cils charmants tenait toute son âme

Et son cœur était vain comme un regard joyeux.
D'autres comme la mer si changeante et si douce
Nous égaraient vers l'âme enfouie en ses yeux
Comme en ces soirs marins où l'inconnu nous pousse.

Mer des yeux sur tes eaux claires nous naviguâmes
Le désir gonflait nos voiles si rapiécées
Nous partions oublieux des tempêtes passées
Sur les regards à la découverte des âmes.

Tant de regards divers, les âmes si pareilles
Vieux prisonniers des yeux nous sommes bien déçus
Nous aurions dû rester à dormir sous la treille
Mais vous seriez parti même eussiez-vous tout su

Pour avoir dans le cœur ces yeux pleins de promesses
Comme une mer le soir rêveuse de soleil
Vous avez accompli d'inutiles prouesses
Pour atteindre au pays de rêve qui, vermeil,

Se lamentait d'extase au-delà des eaux vraies
Sous l'arche sainte d'un nuage cru prophète
Mais il est doux d'avoir pour un rêve ces plaies
Et votre souvenir brille comme une fête.

Time erases the closeness of evening
My hands on her neck as virgin as snow
Her gaze down my nerves in an arpeggio
As over us spring sets its censors swinging

Others, otherwise happy women, have eyes
That, like their griefs, run dark and vast
The dread of night, of evening's demise
Holds the soul between each charming lash

And her heart as empty as her look was gay
Others as soft and shiftless as the sea
Led us to soul in her eyes astray
As through a maritime twilight, the unknown leads

Oceanic eyes, we've sailed your crystal shoals
Desire launching our ragged sails aloft
Unmindful of previous storms, we set off
Across gazes hoping to discover souls

The gazes so varied, yet the souls all one.
Old prisoners of eyes, we were roundly deceived
We should have stayed under arbors, soundly asleep
Though had you known, you still would have gone

To have such promising eyes in your heart
Like an evening sea dreaming up the sun
You've skillfully practiced your pointless arts
To reach rosy lands of dreams that moan

Beyond the true waters in ecstasy aloud
Below the holy ark of a prophetic cloud
How sweet, instead of dreams, these wounds laid bare
And your memory blazing like a country fair.

6

Poésie

À Gustave L. de W.

« Amants, heureux amants! » (La Fontaine)

L'amour monte des cœurs une odeur de roses !
Il est beau de connaître un cœur empli d'amour,
De voir jusqu'en leur fond ses sources larges écloses
Qui vont si vite et clair par cet éclatant jour.
Pourtant les Cœurs aimants ressemblent beaucoup mieux
À la nuit exaltante encor plus que le jour,
À la nuit, claire ou noire, et qui verse des cieux
Un trouble doux, mystérieux comme l'amour.

La nuit ! la mer ! les deux seules choses magiques !
Serré dans son manteau magnifique et soyeux,
Je m'y perds en noyant mes regards dans ses yeux,
Ses yeux indifférents, langoureux et mystiques.

6

POETRY

TO GUSTAVE L. DE W.

"Lovers, happy lovers!" (La Fontaine)

Love draws from the heart a scent of roses!
It is beautiful to know a heart full of love,
To see to the depths of its wide gushing waters
That flow so fast and clear in the light from above.
And yet loving hearts resemble much more
The exhilarating night than the light of the day,
The night, clear or black, that from the sky pours
A soft turmoil, as mysterious as love.

The two magical things: the sea! the night skies!
Wrapped in her coat of magnificent silk,
I am lost as I drown my gaze in her eyes,
Her indifferent, langorous, mystical eyes.

7

J'eus en ma tête un souffreteux oiseau bizarre
Qui chantait mieux que les sources, que les bois
—Dont nous aimions pourtant les solennelles voix,—
Oiseau mélancolique et quelquefois hilare.

Pour sa faiblesse il me fallait être bien clos
Contre le froid, l'air sale et pluvieux des villes.
En des fleurs il restait près du feu qui rutile
Quand l'hiver déroulait ses désolés tableaux.

Hélas j'ai trop ouvert la fenêtre et la porte
J'ai cherché l'action, le plaisir, mots obscurs
Quelqu'un était entré, mortel à ses yeux purs.
Qui donc était entré ? La bête chère est morte.

Qui donc était l'oiseau ? Quelle céleste flamme
S'est éteinte, m'a délaissé pour le soleil
Quelquefois, en sursaut réveillé du sommeil
Qu'est notre vie, je me dis : « C'était mon âme. »

L'oiseau sacré c'est notre poète, notre âme
Notre âme est poésie. Hélas l'oiseau s'est tu !
Somnambules plaintifs caressés ou battus
Vers quel but courons-nous, oublieux de notre âme ?

7

In my head I housed a bird sickly and bizarre
Who sang better than springs, than forests
—Whose solemn voices we nonetheless adore,—
Bird melancholy and sometimes smiling.

To shield your frailty I shut myself tightly
Against the frost, the filthy air and village rain.
Flowering, my bird stayed near the fire that rustled
When winter unrolled its desolate tableaux.

Alas I opened too wide the window and door
I sought action, pleasure, obscure words
Someone entered, deadly to the bird's pure gaze.
Who barged in? My dear beast died.

Who was this bird? What celestial flame
Extinguished itself, abandoned me for the sun—
Sometimes, waking startled from the slumber
That makes up our life, I tell myself: "It was my soul."

The sacred bird is our poet, our soul
Our soul *is* poetry. Alas o bird self-slain!
Somnambulists plaintive caressed or battered
Toward what verse-goal do we race, oblivious to our soul?

8

SUR UNE DEMOISELLE QUI REPRÉSENTA CETTE NUIT LA REINE CLÉOPÂTRE, POUR LE PLUS GRAND TROUBLE ET LA FUTURE DAMNATION D'UN JEUNE HOMME QUI ÉTAIT LÀ.

ET SUR LA DOUBLE ESSENCE MÉTAPHYSIQUE DE LADITE DEMOISELLE.

Peut-être autant que vous Cléopâtre était belle
Mais elle était sans âme : elle était le tableau,
Inconscient gardien d'une grâce immortelle
Qui sans l'avoir compris réalise le Beau.

Tel encor est ce ciel en sa grise harmonie,
Il nous ferait pleurer tant il est triste et las,
Il exprime le doute et la mélancolie
    Et ne les ressent pas !

Vous avez détrôné la reine égyptienne
Vous êtes à la fois l'artiste et l'œuvre d'art.
Votre esprit est profond comme votre regard,
Pourtant nulle beauté lors n'égalait la sienne.

Ses cheveux sentaient bon comme les fleurs des champs ;
J'eusse aimé voir briller sur ses chairs tant aimées
Le long déroulement des tresses embaumées.
Sa parole était lente et douce comme un chant,

8

ON A MAIDEN WHO TONIGHT THE ROLE OF QUEEN CLEOP TO THE GREAT ANXIETY AND FUTURE DAMNATION OF A YOUNG MAN WHO WAS THERE.

AND ON THE DUAL METAPHYSICAL ESSENCE OF SAID MAIDEN.

Perhaps Cleopatra had so lovely a face
But she had no soul: In portrait she'll stay
The unconscious guardian of immortal grace
'Though unaware that she embodies Beauty.

And the sky even more so in its gray harmony
Would make us cry, sad and listless,
It expresses doubt and melancholy
        And couldn't care less!

You have surely dethroned the Egyptian Queen
You are at once artist and work of art.
Your spirit is deep, as is your regard,
'Though no beauty like hers was ever seen.

Like flowers in a field, her hair held a scent,
I'd have loved to see shining on that fancied flesh
The long unfurling of her fragrant tresses.
Her speech lingered, and was soft as a song,

Ses yeux brillaient dans un fond de nacres humides,
Elle arrêtait son corps en des poses languides . . .
Vous avez détrôné la reine de Cydnus.

Vous êtes une fleur et vous êtes une âme.
Nul penser n'habitait son front ceint de lotus,
Ce n'est déjà pas si gracieux pour une femme.

Her eyes lay deep in moist, nacreous sheen,
Her body was held in such languid pose . . .
You have surely dethroned Cydnus's queen.

You are a soul and you are a flower.
No thought ever dwelled in her lotus-bound brow,
In woman a trait one would truly not favor.

9

Madame il peut que j'oublie
Votre divin profil d'oiseau
Et que je crève ma folie
Comme on saute dans un cerceau
Mais vos yeux au plafond de ma tête
Luiront comme des lustres clairs.

9

Madame, it's possible that I have forgotten
Your divine and birdlike profile,
That I have pushed past my own madness
Like one jumping through a hoop,
But always still your eyes will shine
Like bright chandeliers on the ceiling of my mind.

Comme en la claire cour de l'exquis monastère . . .

Ton charme est une cour de joli monastère
Le ciel est bleu de mer entre les arceaux blancs
Il fait bon y passer les chauds jours somnolents
Sous un grêle pilier, boire frais et se taire.

Demain, je le sais bien, devenu solitaire
Éperdument j'irai vers des palais troublants
Mais aujourd'hui ton charme est mon ami ; les lents
Regards de ton œil mauve sont tout pour moi sur terre

Ton front n'enferme pas en sa mince blancheur
L'ombre infinie [d]'où jaillira la lumière
Je t'aime étrangement pourtant, ô tête chère.

Quand à ton rire clair ne battra plus mon cœur
Je rougirai peut-être encore à la douceur
Que c'eût été de rester blotti dans ton cœur.

Comme en la claire cour de l'exquis monastère.

In That Exquisite Monastery's Bright Courtyard . . .

Your charm is the courtyard of a pretty monastery,
The sky sea-blue through its white archways,
Here it is good to spend the hot, sleepy days
Beneath a spindly column, with a cool silent drink.

Tomorrow, I know too well, I will slink
Toward troubling palaces, alone in a daze,
But today your charm is my friend: the slow gaze
Of your mauve eye is all there is on earth, I think.

In its slender whiteness, your brow does not conceal
That infinite shadow from which light will spill,
And yet, dear one, what a strange love I feel.

When my heart no longer beats at your clear laugh
I will perhaps blush at the sweetness still
That it would be to stay curled up in your heart,

In that exquisite monastery's bright courtyard.

II

Sonnet

Si vous avez prédit, si vous avez connu
Dans la douceur tardive et l'orgueil manifeste
L'heure de l'arrivée et le retour du ceste
Ne pleurez pas, le lys ouvert s'est souvenu.

Ne pleurez pas, le raisin mûr est soutenu
Par la chaleur du vin et la colonne agreste
Du cep qui l'encourage et l'élève du geste
Ne pleurez pas, celui qu'on attend est venu.

Les larmes, même d'or, laissez-les aux soleils
Qui durent se coucher aux flots où nulle toile
Ne faisait espérer le retour de la voile

Où, le matin venu dans leur tendre sommeil,
Ils avaient enclos leurs maternelles alarmes
À ceux-là seuls, et même d'or, laissez les larmes.

11

SONNET

If you have foreseen, if you have known
In its belated sweetness and open pride
The arrival time, the counterpunch of the glove
Don't cry, the blooming lily remembers.

Don't cry, the ripe grape is propped
By the wine's heat and the vine's wild column
That nudges it along, raising it to flourish.
Don't cry, the one you've been waiting for has come.

Tears, even golden tears, leave to suns
That sleep on the waves when no canvas comes
Expecting the sail's return.

When morning enters their tender sleep
They hide their motherly fears
To these alone, leave your tears, even your golden tears.

12

Si las d'avoir souffert, plus las d'avoir aimé
La vie après m'avoir de ses lointains charmé
Resserre autour de moi son cercle monotone
Et mon rêve sentant son horizon fermé
Mélancoliquement se replie et s'étonne
Qui sait en écoutant l'automne si touchant
S'il étouffe un sanglot ou s'il retient un chant
Aussi grave que l'heure et comme elle équivoque
Mon cœur sans le savoir franchissait un tournant.

12

So tired of having suffered, more tired of having loved.
Life, having charmed me with its open spaces,
Now tightens around me its monotonous glove,
And my dream, seeing the walls around it rise,
Curls up in melancholy surprise.
Who knows, on hearing the touching sounds of fall,
Whether it is stifling a sob or holding a song at bay,
As solemn as time and, like time, equivocal?
My heart, without knowing it, has turned away.

Laissez pleurer mon cœur entre vos mains fermées
Le ciel décoloré se fane lentement
La fleur de vos yeux clairs comme un apaisement
Abaisse sur mon cœur ses corolles charmées.

Que vos genoux me soient la couche pacifique,
Vêtu de vos regards, j'aurai chaud pour la nuit
Et votre souffle écartera veilleur magique
Tout ce qui souille et ce qui raille et ce qui nuit.

Le port, les champs sont noirs ; après le jour moqueur
La consolante nuit vient de larmes trempée
Et fondant de douceur la brume dissipée
Les feux de ton désir s'allument dans mon cœur.

13

In your closed hands, let my heart cry.
Colors seep from the wilting skies.
The reassuring flower of your clear eye—
In my heart its charmed corolla lies.

May your knees be the bed on which I alight,
Dressed in your gaze, I am warm for the night.
Your breath a magic watchman to sound the alarms
Against all that soils or jeers or harms.

The port, the fields are dark; after the mocking day
Comes consoling night, drenched with tears,
As, melting with sweetness, the fog clears.
And the flames of your desire carry my heart away.

14

ACROSTICHE INACHEVÉ

Instruit par le malheur que vous avez causé
Ne . . .
Cherchez un autre cœur aussi fidèle et tendre
Le mien se réjouira quand vous l'aurez trouvé,
Encore hier en flamme il est hélas en cendre
Mais veut du moins pour vous ce grand bonheur rêvé
Et que, comme un méchant, vous seul avez brisé
Notre malheur fera du bonheur pour un autre
Tâchez instruit . . .

14

UNFINISHED ACROSTIC

Misfortune's your subject and you've taught me well
Er . . .
Register a new heart, one as faithful and tender
'Cause mine will rejoice when you find a new pupil
It was burning just yesterday, but now's a gray cinder,
Loveless, it still wishes you a happy ending without
End, not like ours, which you wrecked like a lout
Someone, no doubt, will profit from our misfortune
Since you're at pains to instruct . . .

Sur ce coteau normand établis ta retraite
Guerrier fou ou bien toi pauvre amoureux vieilli
Parmi les calmes pins viens te fixer au faîte
D'où tu verras la mer sombre et le ciel pâli.
Le vent de mer s'y mêle à l'odeur des feuillées
Et du lait. Tu verras entre deux fins rameaux
Une barque qui boite et par les soirs si beaux
Tu rêveras longtemps des voiles en allées
À l'invisible au loin des lamentables eaux
Et des retours déçus aux ports mélancoliques,
Du retour des vaisseaux dans les soirs magnifiques,
    Luxe et misère et ce sanglot : ton chant
    Parmi les pompes du couchant
Ou dans l'arc triomphal de ces ciels glorieux
N'es-tu pas le vaincu qui suit le char de gloire
    Et qui doit mourir et qui pleure?
Mais la mer ne tait pas sa plainte en harmonie
    Avec la tienne
    Et de cette harmonie naîtra le calme.
Au milieu des rameaux frais et comme des palmes
Au port mélancolique assemble tes espoirs.

15

On this Normandy hillside set your shelter
Mad warrior, poor lover burdened by age—
Amidst calm pines, from a great height
You'll see the sea darken and the sky grow light.
A sea wind mixes the scent of leaves
And milk. There between two delicate boughs
You'll glimpse a trembling boat, come lovely night
You'll dream of sails in flight to an invisible shore,
Far from these waters of lamentation
And dreary returns to sad ports,
As ships turn in night's magnificence
      Rich and miserable sobbing—
      Your song in the pomp of sunset
Or in the triumphal arc of glorious skies.
Aren't you the vanquished one, trailing the chariot of glory
      The one who must die, and who weeps?
But the sea will not still its lament, in harmony
      With your own
      And out of this concord will come great calm.
In the midst of cool branches as a palm tree might
In a sad port, gather all your hopes together.

Si la femme stupide ou détestable est belle
Souviens-toi d'une pour que ton dépit revive.
Son cœur de cendre était dans un corps tout en fleurs.
En une douceur bleue alanguie et plaintive
Ses yeux se repentaient des crimes de son cœur.
Son corps, riche harmonie, inentendu par elle
Chantait ainsi qu'un vers au rythme souple et lent
Faisant rêver d'un art subtil et très puissant
Mais elle eût préféré d'autre esthétique ? Quelle ?
Torches brûlez ! la femme, olivier ou basalte,
Ne ment pour la durée où la flamme s'exalte.
Torches de gloire de par les bûchers d'amour
Vous n'êtes pas l'orgueil que mentit l'amant pour
Égaler son plaisir à la seule pensée !
Votre gloire par les sages vous soit laissée :
Telle une nuit sans nuée, une femme sans voile
Puisque la Lorelie en suif et malgré tout étoile !—
Homme la foi t'élève ou l'amour te prosterne
Ton œil qu'il luise en astre ou comme une eau soit terne
Ne ment pas au désir d'une source éternelle.

If the vile, stupid woman is fair
Think of one: she'll rekindle your spite.
Ashen heart lurked within budding grove
And in tender blue, languid and light,
Her eyes wept the crimes of her heart.
Her form, song neglected and rich,
Slid like poetry, slow and supple,
Raising dreams of an art strong and subtle,
But would she choose a different style? Which?
Torches, burn! Woman, olive or basalt,
Will not lie while the fire burns hot.
Glory's torches: love's pyre, you're not
The pride that the failed lover feigned to
Make his pleasure live up to desire.
May your glory by the sages be left you:
Like eves without mist, or woman sans veil—
Since Lorelei despite the stars is coarse!—
Faith lifts you or love strikes you down.
Your eye, gleaming or dull like stale pools,
Lies not, seeking an eternal source.

PORTRAITS DE PEINTRES
ET DE MUSICIENS

PORTRAITS OF PAINTERS
AND MUSICIANS

ALBERT CUYP I

Cuyp, soleil déclinant dissous dans l'air limpide
Qu'un vol de ramiers gris trouble comme de l'eau,
Moiteur d'or, nimbe au front d'un bœuf ou d'un bouleau,
Encens bleu des beaux jours fumant sur le coteau,
Ou marais de clarté stagnant dans le ciel vide.
Des cavaliers sont prêts, plume rose au chapeau,
Paume au côté ; l'air vif qui fait rose leur peau,
Enfle légèrement leurs fines boucles blondes,
Et, tentés par les champs ardents, les fraîches ondes,
Sans troubler par leur trot les bœufs dont le troupeau
Rêve dans un brouillard d'or pâle et de repos,
Ils partent respirer ces minutes profondes.

Albert Cuyp I

The sinking sun dissolves into air so clear
a flight of doves ripples it like a pond;
a sort of halo gilds birches, gilds bulls!
while bluish incense blurs the hillside, and
splendid quagmires stagnate in the sky.
Riders, mount! Pink plumes are tossed
by gusts that swell the prodigal blond curls
and bring the same pink to every cheek.
Lured by glowing fields and creeks, they trot
past indifferent herds of oxen wrapped
in a golden mist of sleep—galloping now,
breathing the timeless minutes, breathing deep.

ALBERT CUYP II

Cuyp, soleil déclinant dissous dans l'air limpide
Qu'un vol de Goëland trouble comme de l'eau
Moiteur d'or, auréole aux voiles d'un bateau
Au front des bœufs couchés, au ras des flots sans ride.
Des cavaliers sont prêts plume rose au chapeau
Les deux poings sur la hanche et sous leurs boucles
    blondes
Ils regardent les champs ardents, les fraîches ondes
Et passant l'étrier les cuisses au pommeau
Partent pour savourer ces minutes profondes.

Albert Cuyp II

The sinking sun dissolves into air so clear
a flight of gulls ripples it like a pond,
aureoling with identical gold
the sails of a tethered sloop and oxen free
to sleep on the mirroring brink. Riders, mount!
Fists at their hips, and under pale blond curls
eyes on the glowing fields, stirrups slipped
and legs crossed on the pommel, they trot off
to take their trivial pleasure in a timeless hour.

PAULUS POTTER

Sombre chagrin des ciels uniformément gris,
Plus triste d'être bleus aux rares éclaircies,
Et qui laissent alors sur les plaines transies
Filtrer les tièdes pleurs d'un soleil incompris ;
Potter, mélancolique humeur des plaines sombres
Qui s'étendent sans fin, sans joie et sans couleur,
Les arbres, le hameau ne répandent pas d'ombres.
Les maigres jardinets ne portent pas de fleur.
Un laboureur tirant des seaux rentre, et, chétive,
Sa jument résignée, inquiète, et rêvant,
Anxieuse, dressant sa cervelle pensive,
Hume d'un souffle court le souffle fort du vent.

PAULUS POTTER

Sad distress of skies routinely gray,
the sadder for a few blue intervals
which, sudden over sodden fields, release
an unaccustomed sun's indifferent rays;
Potter, mage of these impassive plains
subdued to the horizon—underneath
your village trees no shade, and not one bloom
in your ungrateful gardens. Lugging pails,
a plowman trudges home, his scrawny mare,
resigned yet restive, eager for the barn,
tosses her head, showing the whites of her eyes,
and skittishly sniffs the unrelenting wind.

ANTOINE WATTEAU

Crépuscule grimant les arbres et les faces,
Avec son manteau bleu, sous son masque incertain ;
Poussière de baisers autour des bouches lasses . . .
Le vague devient tendre, et le tout près, lointain.

La mascarade, autre lointain mélancolique,
Fait le geste d'aimer plus faux, triste et charmant.
Caprice de poète—ou prudence d'amant,
L'amour ayant besoin d'être orné savamment—
Voici barques, goûters, silences et musique.

20

ANTOINE WATTEAU

Twilight staining faces under the trees
with its blue cape, its dubious mask,
the dust of kisses round exhausted mouths . . .
What's vague is tender now, what's near, remote.

The masquerade, another sad escape,
misquotes love's gestures—winsome, woebegone—
a poet's whim? a gallant's vigilance?
Love requires a careful staging: here
boats and picnics, music, silences.

ANTON VAN DYCK

Douce fierté des cœurs, grâce noble des choses,
Qui brillent dans les yeux, les velours et les bois ;
Beau langage élevé du maintien et des poses
Héréditaire orgueil des femmes et des rois !

Tu triomphes, Van Dyck, prince des gestes calmes,
Dans tous les êtres beaux qui vont bientôt mourir,
Dans toute belle main qui sait encor s'ouvrir . . .
Sans s'en douter, qu'importe, elle te tend les palmes !

Halte de cavaliers sous les pins, près des flots
Calmes comme eux, comme eux bien proches des sanglots ;
Enfants royaux déjà magnifiques et graves,
Vêtements résignés, chapeaux à plumes braves,
Et bijoux en qui pleure, onde à travers les flammes,
L'amertume des pleurs dont sont pleines les âmes,
Trop hautaines pour les laisser monter aux yeux ;
Et toi par-dessus tous, promeneur précieux
En chemise bleu pâle, une main à la hanche,
Dans l'autre un fruit feuillu détaché de la branche,
Je rêve sans comprendre à ton geste et tes yeux :
Debout mais reposé dans cet obscur asile
Duc de Richmond, Ô jeune sage !—ou charmant fou?—
Je te reviens toujours . . .— Un saphir à ton cou
À des feux aussi doux que ton regard tranquille.

ANTON VAN DYCK

Pride of hearts, the proud grace of substance
shining in velvet, in veneers, in every eye;
the fine high language of posture and of pose,
inherited hauteur of women and of kings!

You triumph, Van Dyck, prince of mild gestures,
in each of these splendid creatures soon to die,
these lovely hands ready, even now, to open—
without a qualm she spreads her palms to you!

Under pines these riders halt beside a brook
calm like them, yet like them close to sobs;
magnificent royal children already grave—
their raiment resigned, their plumed hats mutinous,
and in their jewels glittering, as if through flames,
the bitterness of tears that fill imperious souls,
but not so full as to fall from a single eye.
And you above all, so delicate on parade
in pale-blue silk, one hand forgotten on your hip,
the other holding a pear torn from its branch—
what do they mean, your gesture and your gaze
as you stand so at ease in your dim hideaway,
Your Grace, the Duke of Richmond, O young sage!
—or young fool? Each time it's to you I return,
and each time the sapphire at your throat
glistens as flawless as your unruffled gaze.

22

CHOPIN

Chopin, mer de soupirs, de larmes, de sanglots
Qu'un vol de papillons sans se poser traverse
Jouant sur la tristesse ou dansant sur les flots.
Rêve, aime, souffre, crie, apaise, charme ou berce,
Toujours tu fais courir entre chaque douleur
L'oubli vertigineux et doux de ton caprice
Comme les papillons volent de fleur en fleur ;
De ton chagrin alors ta joie est la complice :
L'ardeur du tourbillon accroît la soif des pleurs.
De la lune et des eaux pâle et doux camarade,
Prince du désespoir ou grand seigneur trahi,
Tu t'exaltes encore, plus beau d'être pâli,
Du soleil inondant ta chambre de malade
Qui pleure à lui sourire et souffre de le voir . . .
Sourire du regret et larmes de l'Espoir !

CHOPIN

Ocean of sighs, and just above the waves
a flight of butterflies pauses . . . no, passes,
circling above the melancholy sea . . .
Dream, love, suffer, sleep it off!
And between each throb of pain produce
the sudden oblivion of your whim—
don't butterflies proceed from flower to flower?
Thus your joy becomes your grief's accomplice
(the whirlpool's thirst is only for more tears).
Prince of despair? A noble lord betrayed?
The moon's pale companion and the sea's,
you still exult, the paler the handsomer,
in the sun that floods your sickroom, weeping
at your smile and suffering at the sight . . .
the smile is for Regret, the tears for Hope!

GLUCK

Temple à l'Amour, à l'Amitié, temple au Courage
Qu'une marquise a fait élever dans son parc
Anglais, où maint amour Watteau bandant son arc
Prend des cœurs glorieux pour cibles de sa rage.

Mais l'artiste allemand—qu'elle eût rêvé de Cnide !—
Plus grave et plus profond, sculpta sans mignardise
Les Amants et les Dieux que tu vois sur la frise :
Hercule a son bûcher dans les jardins d'Armide !

Les talons en dansant ne frappent plus l'allée
Où la cendre des yeux et du sourire éteints
Assourdit nos pas lents et bleuit les lointains ;
La voix des clavecins s'est tue ou s'est fêlée . . .

Mais votre cri muet, Admète, Iphigénie,
Nous terrifie encore, proféré par un geste
Et fléchi par Orphée ou bravé par Alceste
Le Styx,—sans mâts ni ciel—où mouilla ton génie.

Gluck aussi comme Alceste a vaincu par l'Amour
La mort inévitable aux caprices d'un âge ;
Il est debout, auguste temple du Courage,
Sur les ruines du petit temple à l'Amour.

GLUCK

Temple to Love, to Friendship, temple to Courage
That a marquise erected in her English park,
Where drawing his bow Watteau takes many a mark
From glorious hearts as targets of his rage.

But the German artist—Knidos was in her dreams!—
More severe, more profound, carved with ease
The Lovers and Gods you see on the frieze:
Hercules has his pyre beside Armida's streams!

Dancing heels no longer strike the tracks
Where the ash of a smile and dull eyes
Muffles our slow steps and blues the skies;
The voice of the harpsicords dies or it cracks . . .

But Admetus, Iphigenia, your silent cry still terrifies
Us, echoed in a gesture and in the Styx, where
Your genius anchored, where Orpheus had to falter
Though Alcestis braved it without mast or sky.

Gluck like Alcestis was conquered by love
Death inevitable to the vagaries of an age;
He stands, noble temple of Courage,
Above the ruins of a small temple to Love.

SCHUMANN

Du vieux jardin dont l'amitié t'a bien reçu,
Entends garçons et nids qui sifflent dans les haies,
Amoureux las de tant d'étapes et de plaies,
Schumann, soldat songeur que la guerre a déçu.

La brise heureuse imprègne, où passent des colombes,
De l'odeur du jasmin l'ombre du grand noyer,
L'enfant lit l'avenir aux flammes du foyer,
Le nuage ou le vent parle à ton cœur des tombes.

Jadis tes pleurs coulaient aux cris du carnaval
Ou mêlaient leur douceur à l'amère victoire
Dont l'élan fou frémit encor dans ta mémoire ;
Tu peux pleurer sans fin : Elle est à ton rival.

Vers Cologne le Rhin roule ses eaux sacrées.
Ah ! que gaiement les jours de fête sur ses bords
Vous chantiez !—Mais brisé de chagrin, tu t'endors . . .
Il pleut des pleurs dans des ténèbres éclairées.

Rêve où la morte vit, où l'ingrate a ta foi,
Tes espoirs sont en fleurs et son crime est en poudre.
Puis éclair déchirant du réveil où la foudre
Te frappe de nouveau pour la première fois.

Coule, embaume, défile aux tambours ou sois belle !
Schumann, Ô confident des âmes et des fleurs,
Entre tes quais joyeux fleuve saint des douleurs,
Jardin pensif, affectueux, frais et fidèle,
Où se baisent les lys, la lune et l'hirondelle,
Armée en marche, enfant qui rêve, femme en pleurs !

SCHUMANN

In the old garden where friendship hailed you from afar,
Listen to young men and nests that whistle in the hedges,
To lovers weary of so many wounds and false pledges,
Schumann, pensive soldier disappointed by war.

Where doves pass overhead, happy breezes impart
The shadow of the great walnut with the odor of jasmine,
The child reads the future in a flaming shrine,
The cloud or the wind speaks of graves to your heart.

Once your tears flowed toward the cries of the carnival
Or they mingled softness with bitter victory,
Whose mad spirit still trembles in your memory;
You can cry forever: She belongs to your rival.

The Rhine rolls its sacred waters toward Cologne.
Ah! how happily you sang during feast days
On its banks!—But chagrined, you fell into a doze . . .
Tears rained down on the dark alone.

Dream where the dead live, where the doubter has trust,
Your hopes are in flower and your crime is dust.
Then the heartrending flash of waking when
Lightning strikes you for the first time again.

Flow, embalm, march to the drums or be beautiful!
Schumann, O confidant of flowers and hollows,
Holy river of pain between your joyous shores,
Pensive garden, affectionate, fresh and faithful,
Where the lilies kiss, the moon and the swallows,
Army on the move, infant who dreams, woman in tears!

MOZART

Italienne aux bras d'un Prince de Bavière
Dont l'œil triste et glacé s'enchante à sa langueur !
Dans ses jardins frileux il tient contre son cœur
Ses seins mûris à l'ombre, où téter la lumière.

Sa tendre âme allemande,—un si profond soupir !—
Goûte enfin la paresse ardente d'être aimée,
Il livre aux mains trop faibles pour le retenir
Le rayonnant espoir de sa tête charmée.

Chérubin, Don Juan ! loin de l'oubli qui fane
Debout dans les parfums tant il foula de fleurs
Que le vent dispersa sans en sécher les pleurs
Des jardins andalous aux tombes de Toscane !

Dans le parc allemand où brument les ennuis,
L'Italienne encore est reine de la nuit.
Son haleine y fait l'air doux et spirituel

Et sa Flûte enchantée égoutte avec amour
Dans l'ombre chaude encor des adieux d'un beau jour
La fraîcheur des sorbets, des baisers et du ciel.

25

MOZART

Italian lady in the arms of a Bavarian knight
Whose sad and chilly gaze rejoices in her lazy art!
He holds her ripened breasts to his heart
In the shade of his shivering gardens, to feed on light.

His tender German soul—such a deep sigh!—
Tastes the ardent idleness of being loved at last,
He hands the radiant hope of his charmed past
To hands too feeble to lift it high.

Cherubino, Don Juan! Far from the fading oblivion
Standing amid the aromas he trampled so many flowers
That the wind scattered without drying his tears
From the tombs of Tuscany to the Andalusian garden!

In the German park where troubles spread like vapor,
The Italian lady is still queen of the night.
Her breath makes the air there holy and delicate

And her enchanted flute drips with ardor
Still warm in the shade, the farewells of a lovely day
The freshness of heaven, of kisses, of sorbet.

MÉLANGES

MISCELLANY

26

Pour la Revue Lilas.

Sous réserve de destruction ultérieure.

À mon cher ami Jacques Bizet.

Quinze ans. 7 heures du soir. Octobre.

Le ciel est d'un violet sombre marqué de taches luisantes. Toutes les choses sont noires. Voici les lampes, l'horreur des choses usuelles.

Elles m'oppressent. La nuit qui tombe comme un couvercle noir ferme l'espoir, grand ouvert au jour, d'y échapper. Voici l'horreur des choses usuelles, et l'insomnie des premières heures du soir, pendant qu'au-dessus de moi on joue des valses et que j'entends le bruit crispant des vaisselles remuées dans une pièce voisine . . .

Dix-sept ans. 11 heures du soir. Octobre.

La lampe illumine faiblement les recoins sombres de ma chambre et met un grand rond de lumière vive, où entrent ma main, tout d'un coup ambrée, mon livre, mon bureau. Aux murs bleuissent de minces filets de lune entrés par l'imperceptible écartement des tentures rouges. Tout le monde est couché dans le grand appartement silencieux . . .—J'entrouve la fenêtre pour revoir une dernière fois la douce face fauve, bien ronde, de la lune amie. J'entends comme l'haleine très fraîche, froide, de toutes les choses qui dorment—l'arbre d'où suinte de la lumière bleue—de la belle lumière bleue transfigurant au loin par une échappée de rues, comme un paysage polaire électriquement il-luminé, les pavés bleus et pales. Par-dessus s'étendent les infinis

26

FOR THE REVUE LILAS.

SUBJECT TO EVENTUAL
DESTRUCTION.

For my dear friend Jacques Bizet.

Fifteen years old. 7 o'clock in the evening. October.

The sky is a dark violet marked with gleaming patches. Each thing is black. Here are the lamps, the horror of everyday things. They oppress me. Night, coming down like a black cover, closes off hope, wide open to the day, from escaping into it. Here is the horror of everyday things, and the insomnia of the first hours of the evening, while above me they are playing waltzes and I can hear the irritating noise of dishes being moved in a neighboring room . . .

Seventeen years old. 11 o'clock in the evening. October.

The lamp weakly illuminates the dark corners of my room and casts a wide circle of bright light over my hand, suddenly amber-colored, my book, my desk. On the walls, slender fillets of moonlight turn blue, having entered through the imperceptible parting of the red curtains. Everyone is in bed, in the great silent apartment . . .—I open the window a little to look one more time on the gentle wild face, full and round, of my friend the moon. I hear something like the very fresh, cold breath of every sleeping thing—the tree sweating blue light—the lovely blue light transfiguring, in the distance, through a gap in the streets, like an electrically illuminated polar landscape, the pale blue pavingstones. Up above extend the infinite blue fields ablossom with frail stars . . .—I have closed the window. I have gone

champs bleus où fleurissent de frêles étoiles . . .—J'ai refermé la fenêtre. Je suis couché. Ma lampe posée près de mon lit sur une tablette, au milieu de verres, de flacons, de boissons fraîches, de petits livres précieusement reliés, de lettres d'amitié ou d'amour, éclaire vaguement dans le fond ma bibliothèque. L'heure divine ! Les choses usuelles, comme la nature, je les ai sacrées, ne pouvant les vaincre. Je les ai vêtues de mon âme et d'images intimes ou splendides. Je vis dans un sanctuaire, au milieu d'un spectacle. Je suis le centre des choses et chacune me procure des sensations et des sentiments magnifiques ou mélancoliques, dont je jouis. J'ai devant les yeux des visions splendides. Il fait doux dans ce lit . . . Je m'endors.

to bed. My lamp, placed next to my bed on a shelf amid glasses, bottles, cool drinks, little books in precious bindings, friends' letters or love letters, diffusely illuminates my bookcase in the background. The divine hour! Everyday things, like nature—I have sancified them, since I cannot vanquish them. I have clothed them in my soul and in intimate or splendid images. I live in a sanctuary, in the midst of a spectacle. I am the center of things, and each of them procures me magnificent or melancholy sensations and sentiments in which I delight. I have splendid visions before my eyes. The bed is soft . . . I fall asleep.

Pourquoi j'aime tant les chèvrefeuilles ? C'est parce que mon bien-aimé a planté un chèvrefeuille, sous la fenêtre de ma chambre afin qu'à mon réveil la grisante odeur de ses fleurs me dise : « Toute la nuit les pensées de ton bien-aimé n'ont cessé d'exhaler vers toi leur plus doux parfum d'amour. »

Pourquoi j'aime tant les colchiques d'automne? C'est parce que mon bien-aimé, afin d'en mettre une à mon corsage, s'est, une nuit, jeté dans l'eau. Depuis j'ai toujours gardé la fleur qui me rappelle la nuit où, pour la première fois j'ai compris que pour un de mes regards mon bien-aimé se jetterait dans la rivière.

Pourquoi j'aime tant la blancheur des lys ? C'est parce que mon bien-aimé m'a donné une fleur pure de lys blanc, un soir qu'après m'avoir désirée de tous les désirs de sa vie il comprit que le seul bien ici-bas est la pureté du corps comme la pureté de l'âme, et, revenant de son erreur : « Le désir que j'aurai désormais, m'a-t-il dit, est le seul qui ne changera jamais en désillusion une fois réalisé : c'est le désir de souffrir et de mourir pour mon amour. »

Pourquoi j'aime tant la fleur triste des clématites ? C'est parce que mon bien-aimé s'est tué pour n'avoir pas pu me faire accepter une fleur de clématite. J'ai refusé la fleur qu'il m'offrait car en échange de sa fleur j'aurais dû lui donner mon cœur et j'aime mieux voir mon bien-aimé mort que de voir mon cœur lui appartenir.

Non, mon cœur ne lui a jamais appartenu quoique le sien fut bien à moi. Mon cœur n'appartiendra jamais à personne et je ne sais seulement si j'ai un cœur ; mais je sais bien qu'aucun amour ne saura prendre ma vie car je suis une honnête petite femme ; une honnête petite femme ne doit pas aimer : elle doit faire rire, pleurer et mourir les autres : mais son cœur à elle doit ignorer toute souffrance.

27

Why do I so love the honeysuckle? It is because my beloved has planted a honeysuckle under my bedroom window so that when I wake, the intoxicating smell of its flowers will say to me: "All night long, the thoughts of your beloved have ceaselessly exhaled to you their sweetest scent of love."

Why do I so love the autumn crocus? It is because one night my beloved, so as to be able to put one in my buttonhole, threw himself into the water. Ever since, I have always kept the flower that reminds me of the night when, for the first time, I understood that in return for just one glance from me, my beloved would throw himself into the river.

Why do I so love the whiteness of the lily? It is because my beloved gave me the pure flower of a white lily, one night after having desired me with all the desire of his life, when he understood that the only good thing here on earth is purity of the body, like purity of the soul, and when, seeing his mistake, he said to me: "The desire that I will feel henceforth is the only desire that will never change to disillusionment once I have fulfilled it: it is the desire to suffer and die for my love."

Why do I so love the sad flower of the clematis? It is because my beloved killed himself when he could not make me accept a clematis flower. I refused the flower he offered me because in exchange for his flower I would have had to give him my heart, and I would rather see my beloved dead than see my heart belong to him.

No, my heart never belonged to him, though his heart was certainly mine. My heart will never belong to anyone and I don't even know if I have a heart; but I know well that no love will be able to take my life because I am a decent little woman; a decent little woman does not have to love: she must make others laugh, cry, and die: but her own heart must be unacquainted with all suffering.

Pâles, ainsi qu'on voit aux rares porcelaines
Le rêve d'une mer d'opale près d'Yuldo,
Avril y sourirait sur un fin glacis d'eau
Bien douce avec le ton clair des japoneries,
Un pâle pommier effeuillerait parmi
(En ce pays l'absurde adorable est permis)
Le trésor délicat des pétales chéris.
Dessus miroiterait un vol de blancs phalènes,
D'une nuance exquise et tendre de satin ;
Au ciel s'alanguiraient les roses du matin.

28

With the pallor one sees in rare porcelain
The dream of an opal sea near Yuldo,
April smiling above a fine water glaze
So sweet, with a clear tint of japonerie—
A pale apple tree sheds its leaves
(In this land the adorably absurd is allowed)
The delicate treasure of cherished petals
Sparkles on a flight of white moths,
Exquisite tint, tender as satin
On a sky languid with morning dew.

MAGDA

Imitez votre mère Ida
Dans sa grâce aimable et charmante
Soyez douce, soyez aimante
Ô Mademoiselle Magda.

Horace qui vous ballada
Ce mois-ci souffrit fort de votre humeur méchante
Pour Dieu soyez indulgente
Aux défauts des autres, Magda.

Pour un oui pour un non Magdeleine vida
Sur moi tout le torrent de son fiel détestable
Oh Mademoiselle Magda !

Jamais c'est un bien gros mot pour vos minces lèvres
Mordant des fruits ne sachant que cela,
Quand du chagrin vous comprendrez les fièvres
Revenez sur votre « jamais », chère Magda.

29

MAGDA

Do like your mother Ida
With her grace so charming and upbeat
Be friendly and be sweet
O Miss Magda.

Right now Horace, your balladeer
Suffers unthinkably from your meanness
For God's sake, show some lenience
Toward others' flaws, Magda my dear.

For a big yes, or a no, Magdalene did piss
The full torrent of her hateful
Venom onto me, Oh Magda, dear Miss!

Never, what a big word for such fine lips
Which know nothing but a fruit-biting tease,
One day you'll learn of the shame fever-itch
And regret your "never," *chère* Maggie.

Sans doute Sévigné, Saint-Simon et Voltaire
    Connaissent la couleur
L'histoire la plus éloquente doit se taire
    Et s'incliner devant la leur !

Pourtant parfois Joubert à mon loisir docile
Imprime un plus tendre ressac,
Et puis mon goût ému le quitte, hésite, oscille
Entre Doudan, Pline et Balzac.

30

Saint-Simon, Sevigné, and Voltaire knew the score
    There's no use trying to deny it
The most eloquent history should drop to the floor
    Before them and be quiet!

And yet sometimes Joubert, at my most laid back
    Imprints a more delicate spume
And I leave him for Pliny, Doudan, and Balzac
    Between whom I hesitate, waver, and swoon.

Tu verras, signe indéchiffrable et familier
Ternissant son reflet au couchant qui l'arrose
Le vaincre lentement s'élever et briller
La lune d'or dans le ciel encor rose.

31

You'll see a sign, indecipherable, familiar
Its reflection dulled by a setting sun
That bathes and slowly conquers it, risen brilliance—
Moon of gold in a sky still pink.

32

MENSONGES

*A Léon Delafosse qui, plus merveilleux que le
Roi Midas qui changeait tout en or, change
tout en harmonie, même les vers les plus sordides,
à travers son inspiration et sous ses doigts magiques.*
—Marcel Proust

Si le bleu de l'opale est tendre
Est-ce d'aimer . . . confusément . . . ?
Le clair de lune semble attendre
Un cœur qui saura le comprendre . . .
La Douceur du Ciel bleu sourit au cœur aimant

La douceur du ciel bleu sourit au cœur aimant
Comme un pardon pour sa démence
Dans le ciel est-ce encor la matière qui ment ?
Est-ce déjà Dieu qui commence ?

Si le bleu de vos yeux est triste
Comme un doux regret qui persiste
Est-ce d'aimer ce qui n'existe
Pas en ce monde—Aimer est triste !

Vos yeux vagues, vos yeux avides
Vos yeux profonds, hélas sont vides
Profonds et vides sont les Cieux

Et la tendresse du bleu pâle
Est un mensonge dans l'opale
Et dans le ciel et dans vos yeux.

32

LIES

*To Léon Delafosse who, more marvelous than
King Midas who changed all to gold, changes
all to harmony, even the most sordid verses,
by virtue of his inspiration and beneath his magic fingers.*
—Marcel Proust

If the opal's blue is tender
Is it due to love . . . confusedly?
Moonlight seems to await
A heart that will know how to fathom it . . .
Blue celestial sweetness smiled on a loving heart

Blue celestial sweetness smiled on a loving heart
Like a pardon for its dementia
In the sky is it still Matter that fibs?
Is it always God's fault?

If the blue of your eyes is *triste*
Like a sweet regret that persists
Is it for love of what doesn't exist
In this world—to love is *triste*!

Your vague eyes, your avid eyes
Your profound eyes, alas are vacant
Profound and vacant are the Heavens

And the tenderness of light blue
Is a lie within the opal
Both in the sky and in your eyes.

Lundi à Une Heure

L'insensibilité de la nature entière
Ainsi semble combler le vide de nos cœurs.
C'est un jeu décevant de l'aveugle matière
Dans l'opale et le ciel et les yeux où, vainqueur
Et tour à tour blessé, semblait rêver l'amour.
La forme des cristaux, le pigment des prunelles,
Et l'épaisseur de l'air nous trompent tour à tour,
Essayant de tromper nos douleurs éternelles
À travers la nature, et la femme, et les yeux ;
     Et la tendresse du bleu pâle,
     Est un mensonge dans l'opale
     Et dans le ciel et dans vos yeux.

33

MONDAY, ONE O'CLOCK

The insensibility of nature's entirety
Seems to fill our heart's void.
Blind matter plays a deceptive game
In opal and sky and eyes where, victorious
And wounded by turns, love appears to dream.
The crystal's form, the eye-pupil's pigment,
And the air's thickness trick us bit by bit,
Trying to trump our eternal anguish
Through nature, and woman, and eyes;
  And the tenderness of blue's pallor
  Is a lie within the opal
  And in the sky and in your eyes.

34

Pour l'Album de Mélancolie

Nouveaux Lieds de Macédoine

Lise dit au vieux moine
—J'aime bien Antoine, j'aime bien Antoine
Lise dit au vieux moine
Ses poiriers sont en fleurs

Lisette est tout en pleurs
—J'aime bien Antoine, j'aime bien Antoine
Lisette est tout en pleurs
À cause du vieux moine

Prends dit-elle je meurs
—J'aime bien Antoine, j'aime bien Antoine
Tous mes bijoux, vieux moine
Rubis et calcédoine
Diamant tout en pleurs
Et saphir tout en fleurs.

Prends ta faux de sardoine
—J'aime bien Antoine, j'aime bien Antoine
Et va faner là-bas, sous la rosée en pleurs
Le clair de lune exquis des jacinthes en fleurs

Car dit-elle et je meurs
—J'aime bien Antoine, j'aime bien Antoine
Avant qu'aille l'avoine
Au panier des faucheurs
Les poiriers sont en fleurs

34

For the Album of Melancholy

New Ballads of Macedonia

Lise says to the old monk
—I like Antoine, I like Antoine
Lise says to the old monk
His pear trees are abloom

Lisette sheds tears of gloom
—I like Antoine, I like Antoine
Lisette sheds tears of gloom
Because of the old monk

Take them she says I'm dying
—I like Antoine, I like Antoine
All my jewels, old monk
Ruby and Chalcedon
Diamond tears of gloom
And sapphire all abloom

Take your false sardonyx
—I like Antoine, I like Antoine
And fade there, under a weeping dew
Exquisite moonlight of hyacinths in bloom

Because she says and I'm dying
—I like Antoine, I like Antoine
Before the oats have gone
Into the mowers' baskets
The pear trees are abloom

Car dit-elle et j'en meurs
—J'aime bien Antoine, j'aime bien Antoine
Il sera roi de Macédoine
Il chassera jésuite et moine
Et la carmélite en pleurs
Et soigne en attendant ses beaux poiriers en fleurs.

Because she says and I'll die of it
—I like Antoine, I like Antoine
    He will be king of Macedon
    He'll hunt down monks and Jesuits
    And the Carmelites will weep for it
And waiting, prune his beautiful pear trees abloom

35

Pour l'Album de Mélancolie

Nouveau Lied de France

La bergeronnette—je vois l'améthyste
Se fanait dans l'étang plus triste
La bergeronnette a fait place nette
    Venez belle lurette . . .

Le rossignolet—j'entends la topaze
Qui perle à ton cœur à travers la gaze
Le rossignolet fuit le bois seulet
    Jouons au furet.

Le martin-pêcheur—je baise l'opale
    Dans ton regard pâle
Le martin-pêcheur suit le flot chanteur
    À la Chandeleur

Le rouge-gorge—au flot de l'émeraude
Voit dans un rayon un lutin qui rôde
Si le rouge-gorge a pillé notre orge
Nous la sèmerons avant la Saint-George

La tourterelle—le beau diamant
Brûle et brille de feux comme un amant
La tourterelle a palpité de l'aile
    Sois fidèle

For the Album of Melan

New Ballad of France

Wagtail—I see the amethyst
Fading into the lake of *tristesse*.
The wagtail made a clean sweep of it.
    A long time coming . . .

Nightingale—I hold out the topaz
That beads at your heart through the gauze
The nightingale flees the wood alone
    Let's play pass the parcel

Kingfisher—I kiss the opal
In your pale eyes
The kingfisher follows the waves, singer
    At Candlemass

Robin-redbreast—afloat in the green
Spies in the light an imp who skulks
If the robin has stolen our barley
We sow it before St. George's Day

Turtle Dove, the beautiful diamond
Burning and shining with fire like a lover
The dove fluttered its wing
    Be true

L'oiseau-mouche prend la pierre de lune
Ou bien croit que je la donne à quelqu'une
L'oiseau-mouche au fond d'un œillet se couche
Je te baiserai sur la bouche.

Hummingbird takes the moonstone
Maybe he thinks it's for my special someone
The hummingbird naps in the carnation's depths
    I'm going to kiss you right on the mouth.

DORDRECHT

Ton ciel toujours un peu
    bleu
Le matin souvent un peu
    pleut

Dordrecht endroit si beau
    Tombeau
De mes illusions chéries

Quand j'essaye à dessiner
Tes canaux, tes toits, ton clocher
Je me sens comme aimer
    Des patries

Mais le soleil et les cloches
Ont bien vite resséché
Pour la grand-messe et les brioches
Ton luisant clocher

Ton ciel bleu
Souvent pleut
Mais dessous toujours un peu
Reste bleu.

36

DORDRECHT

Your sky always slightly
    blue
Morning often slightly
    wet

Lovely Dordrecht
    Tomb
Of my precious illusions

When I try to draw
Your canals, your roofs, your steeple
I feel I could love
    A homeland.

Still sun and church bells
Dry out quickly
For high mass, also brioches
And gleaming steeple

Your sky
So often wet,
But always underneath
A bit stays blue.

DORDRECHT

Le pâtissier sur la place
 Où seul un pigeon bouge
Reflète sur le canal bleu comme de la glace
 Son grand moule rouge
Un chaland s'avance et dérange
 Un nénuphar et du soleil
Qui dans la glace du pâtissier, fiche le camp sur la tarte
  aux groseilles
 Et fait peur à la mouche qui la mange
Voici la fin de la messe tout le monde sort alleluia Sainte
  Mère des Anges
Allons faire un tour en barque sur le canal après une
  heure de sommeil.

DORDRECHT

A baker in the square
    Where nothing stirs but a pigeon
Reflections in an icy blue canal—
    A great red mould,
A barge slipping forward, disturbing
    A waterlily, sunlight
In the baker's mirror flitting over a red currant
    Tart,
    Scaring hell out of a feasting fly.
At the end of the mass, here comes everybody—alleluia,
    Holy Mother of Angels
Come, let's take a boat ride on the canal
    After a little nap.

38

ÉPITAPHE POUR UN CHIEN

Ici repose ami le beau corps de la bête
Qui tant de mercredis et sans trêve aboya
Nul n'aurait peint—Whistler, Michel-Ange ou Goya
L'horreur de l'Arrivante ayant aux pieds sa tête.

Sois clément que tu sois Athénien ou Gète
Cher étranger pour lui prie Hercule ou Freia
Hélas celui qui sans merci nous effraya
Moins heureux que Beulé n'est plus d'aucune fête.

Que ce soit la Syrinx ou bien le Mirliton
Fais résonner ton chant en l'honneur de Gaston.
Anxieusement je prends ma subtile musette

Car mieux que Germiny, Ganderax ou Brinquand
Ce chien par son aboi longuement éloquent
Réconfortait le cœur de la froide Suzette.

Epitaph for a Dog

Here rests, my friend, the handsome body of the beast
That barked so many Wednesdays without cease.
No one could paint—not Whistler, Michelangelo, or Goya
The horror of a newcomer with its head near his feet.

Whether you're an Athenian or Dacian, be merciful,
Dear stranger. Pray to Hercules or Freya on its behalf.
Less fortunate than Beulé, this beast who mercilessly
Frightened us no longer parties, alas.

Be it with Syrinx or even Mirliton
Sing out your song in honor of Gaston.
Anxiously I take my subtle musette

For better than Germiny, Ganderax, or Brinquand,
With its non-stop eloquent barking
This dog comforted the heart of cold Suzette.

Donc si vous le voulez sans être trop loquace
Madame je ferai ladite dédicace.

Si le noble azur de vos yeux l'ordonna
Madame, si vos yeux exquis de Madonna
Si bleus que l'on dirait—dut enrager plus d'une—
Deux pétales d'iris ou deux rayons de lune,
Ou deux papillons bleus pris aux mailles des cils
Et palpitant encor dans leurs réseaux subtils,
J'obéis à vos yeux délicatement pâles
Ainsi qu'un reflet de pervenche ou les opales
Et dont—pareil à ces morceaux de ciel dans l'eau
Cernés par l'ombre du tilleul ou du bouleau
Qui tremblent longuement si survient le zéphyre—
Le frissonnant azur bouge dans un sourire !

39

If you can live without confabulation
Madame you'll have your dedication.

Should the noble blue of your eyes demand it
Madame, should your Madonnan eyes' exquisite
Blue command it—having crazed not a few—
As two iris petals or two moonbeams do,
Or two blue butterflies by your lashes enmeshed
Bound and pulsing in those delicate nets,
I'll obey your pale pastel eyes, obey
Their opal-periwinkle mirrors' sway,
Like patches of sky on glassy waters
Betrayed by the linden or birch's leafy daughters
Those shadows trembling endlessly if Zephyrs linger—
Which the shivering blue tickles with a smile's finger.

Puisque vous conservez tous ces papiers divers
Je suis obligé de vous écrire en vers
Si vous ne vous sentez pas las
Nationaliste Nicolas
Dans vingt minutes donnez-moi
Un bon café au lait qui fume.

40

Since you always keep these notes diverse,
I am obliged to write in verse,
If you don't feel list-
Less, Nicolas the nationalist,
In twenty minutes give me,
A nice, steamy, milky coffee.

J'écris un opuscule
Par qui Bourget descend
Et Boylesve recule.

41

I wrote a line (or two)
In which Bourget fell
And Boylesve withdrew.

PASTICHES

PASTICHES

PETIT PASTICHE DE
MME DE NOAILLES

Mon cœur sage, fuyez l'odeur des térébinthes
Voici que le matin frise comme un jet d'eau.
L'air est un écran d'or où des ailes sont peintes ;
Pourquoi partiriez-vous pour Nice ou pour Yeddo ?

Quel besoin avez-vous de la luisante Asie
Des monts de verre bleu qu'Hokusaï dessinait
Quand vous sentez si fort la belle frénésie
D'une averse dorant les toits de Vésinet !

Ah ! Partir pour le Pecq, dont le nom semble étrange,
Voir avant de mourir le Mont Valérien
Quand le soigneux couchant se dispose et s'effrange
Entre la Grande Roue et le Puits artésien.

42

A Brief Pastiche of Madame de Noailles

My wise heart, flee the turpentine smell
Here's the morning curling its fresh flow.
The air is a screen of gold, painted wings as well;
Why would you leave for Nice or for Yeddo?

What need have you of gleaming Asia
Or Hokusai's drawing of blue glass mountains
When you can smell so strongly the frenzia
Of the Vésinet roofs rain-gilded in fountains!

Ah, to leave for le Pecq, whose name seems odd,
To see before dying Mount Valerien
When the careful sunset lays itself all frayed
Between the Great Wheel and the well Artesian.

43

ADRESSES

Facteur d'un pied rythmique il faut que tu t'en ailles
Cent neuf, au bout de l'avenue Henri Martin
Porter ce mot à la Comtesse de Noailles
Qu'aiment le mélilot, la carotte et le thym.

Facteur si tu n'es pas un sot
Dans la rue—oui ! Dirait Beaunier-Monceau
Je ne doute pas que tu trouves
En train de lire Sainte-Beuve
Ou Nietche, au 31, la Veuve.

D'un rapide, Ô facteur comme une aile
Vole rue (au) de Grenelle
Remets ce mot à la Fitz-James
Mais sur mon âme éternelle
J'aime encore mieux Francis Jammes.

Facteur ne fais pas joujou
J'ai tracé, relu, signé
Ce mot pour la Chevigné
Sa rue est maintenant (au 10) celle d'Anjou
Facteur tu me sembles loustic . . .

Facteur trouve au 102 du Boulevard Haussmann
Proust qui fut, l'autre siècle, épris de Laure Hayman

Facteur trouve au 102 du Boulevard Haussmann
Un Marcel Proust barbu comme Léandre Helmann

43

ADDRESSES

Postman, with a rhythmic step you must go
To the end of avenue Henri Martin, 109
Carry this word to the Comtesse de Noailles
Who loves sweet clover, carrots, and thyme.

Postman, if it's true that you're no dodo,
On the street—yes! They call it Beaunier-Monceau
I have no doubt that you will find
Reading Sainte-Beuve
Or Nietzsche, at 31, the Widow.

With a speed, O postman like a wing
Fly to the street called (I think) Grenelle
Deliver this note to the Fitz-James
But, on my eternal soul
I have more love for Francis Jammes.

Postman, do not play games
I have outlined, reread, signed
This note for la Chevigné
Her street is now (at #10) the one called Anjou
Postman, you seem quite strange . . .

Postman: find, at 102 Boulevard Haussmann
Proust who was, last century, in love with Laure Hayman

Postman: find, at 102 Boulevard Haussmann
One Marcel Proust, bearded like Léandre Helmann

Marcel Proust (au 102 Boulevard Haussmann)
Se lève—et non pas couche, avec Lilli Lehmann

Marcel Proust, au 102 du Boulevard Haussmann
A quelques qualités, mais l'on préfère Hermann.

Proust habite au 102 du Boulevard Haussmann
Plus ardant pour Ormuz et lassé d'Arriman.

Marcel Proust (of 102 Boulevard Haussmann)
Rises—and does not lie, with Lilli Lehmann

Marcel Proust, of 102 Boulevard Haussmann
Has a few qualities, but most prefer Hermann.

Proust lives at 102 Boulevard Haussmann
Still hot for Ormuz, and over Arriman.

44

Prière du Marquis de Clermont-Tonnerre

(imité de Robert de Montesquiou)

Je greffe les rosiers dont sont fleuris les marbres,
Ceux du Paros « mousseux » et du Carrare « thé »
Et, de ces rosoyants et ces blondissants arbres,
Je sais tirer des chants inconnus d'Hardy-Thé.

Mon pinceau fait courir au rinceaux des abaques
Cet or qui fait marcher, à ce qu'on dit, Cloton !
Trianon, Vézelay, ne sont que des baraques,
Quand l'esprit les compare au palais Lauriston !

Seigneur, si vous daignez m'admettre dans les salles
Où le Juste rompra le Pain Essentiel,
Que de marbre aussi pur étincellent vos stalles !
De Glissolles et d'Ancy, que soit digne le Ciel !

(POUR COPIE CONFORME :
MARCEL PROUST)

(ANNÉE 1910)

44

The Prayer of the Marquis de Clermont-Tonnerre

(after Robert de Montesquiou)

I graft the roses from which flower marble,
Those of sparkling Paros and Carrara tea
And, from those rosy and golden arbors,
I know how to draw the unknown songs of Hardy-Tea.

My paintbrush runs through the foliage of abacuses
That gold that makes things go, as they say, Cloton!
Trianon, Vézelay, nothing but dollhouses,
When the mind compares them to the Palace of Lauriston!

My Lord, if you deign to admit me to those halls
Where the Just break the Essential Leaven,
As pure as the marble that sparkles in your stalls!
Of Glissolles and d'Ancy, who will be worthy of Heaven!

A TRUE COPY:
MARCEL PROUST

1910

45

ÉCHO

Notre ami Marcel Proust, dont les lecteurs du Figaro connaissent les pastiches, a une immense admiration pour le *Pelléas et Mélisande* de Debussy. L'autre jour, il sortait d'une réunion avec un ami qui ne pouvait pas trouver son chapeau. Marcel Proust improvisa le duo suivant. Que le lecteur mette sous les questions le déclamation pressante, rapide, sous les réponses le gravité mélancolique, la mystérieuse cantilène de Debussy, et il sentira la justesse extrême de ce petit pastiche non pas de la pièce de Maeterlinck, mais du livret de Debussy (il y a une nuance).

Markel :   Vous avez eu tort de laisser ce chapeau ! vous ne le retrouverez jamais !

Pelléas :   Pourquoi ne le retrouverai-je pas ?

Markel :   On ne retrouve jamais rien . . . ici . . . Il est perdu pour toujours.

Pelléas :   En nous en allant, nous en prendrons un,—qui lui ressemble !

Markel :   Il n'y en a pas qui lui ressemble !

Pelléas :   Comment était-il donc ?

Markel, *très doucement* :

C'était un pauvre petit chapeau
Comme en porte tout le monde !

Personne n'aurait pu dire de chez qui il venait . . . il avait l'air de venir du bout du monde . . . !
Maintenant il ne faut plus le chercher, car nous ne le retrouverions pas.

45

ECHO

Our friend Marcel Proust, whose pastiches are known to readers of *Le Figaro*, has an immense admiration for "Pelléas and Mélisande" by Debussy. The other day, he left a meeting with a friend who could not find his hat. Marcel Proust improvised the following duet. If the reader places on the questions a rapid, stressed declamation, and on the responses a melancholic gravitas, that mysterious cantilena of Debussy's, he will sense the extreme accuracy of this little pastiche not of Maeterlinck's play, but of Debussy's little book (there is a difference).

Markel:	You were wrong to forget that hat! You will never get it back!
Pelléas:	Why won't I get it back?
Markel:	One never gets anything back . . . here . . . it is lost forever.
Pelléas:	When we leave, we will take one,—that resembles it!
Markel:	There isn't one that resembles it!
Pelléas:	What was it like, then?

Markel, very softly:

It was a sad little hat
Like everyone wears!

Nobody would be able to say to whom it belonged . . . it might as well have come from the ends of the earth . . . !
Now we must not look for it, for we will not find it.

Pelléas :	Il me semble que ma tête commence à avoir froid pour toujours. Il fait un grand froid dehors. C'est l'hiver ! Si encore le soleil n'était pas couché. Pourquoi avait-on laissé la fenêtre ouverte. Il faisait là-dedans une atmosphère lourde et empoisonnée, j'ai cru plusieurs fois que j'allais me trouver mal. Et maintenant tout l'air de toute la terre ...
Markel :	Vous avez, Pelléas, le visage grave et plein de larmes [de] ceux qui se sont enrhumés pour longtemps ! Allons-nous-en. Nous ne le retrouverons pas. Quelqu'un qui n'est pas d'ici l'aura emporté et Dieu sait où il est en ce moment. Il est trop tard. Tous les autres chapeaux sont partis. Nous ne pourrons plus en prendre un autre. C'est une chose terrible, Pelléas.

Mais ce n'est pas votre faute.

Pelléas :	Quel est ce bruit ?
Markel :	Ce sont les voitures qui partent.
Pelléas :	Pourquoi partent-elles ?
Markel :	Nous les aurons effrayées. Elles savaient que nous nous en allions très loin d'ici et elles sont parties. Elles ne reviendront jamais.

Ainsi Marcel Proust divertissait sa mélancolie, tout en retournant travailler à une œuvre considérable qu'on ne connaîtra pas avant l'année prochaine.

Pelléas:	I feel like my head will now be cold forever. It is very cold out. It's winter! If only the sun had not yet gone down. Why did they leave the window open. In here, the atmosphere is heavy and poisonous; I thought several times that I was going to be sick. And now, all the breeze of all the world . . .
Markel:	You have, Pelléas, the hollow, tearful face [of] someone who has been sick for a long time! Let's go, then. We will not get it back. Someone who is not from here will have taken it, and God knows where he is at this moment. It is too late. All the other hats have gone. We cannot take another. It's a terrible thing, Pelléas.

But it's not your fault.

Pelléas:	What is that noise?
Markel:	It's the cars leaving.
Pelléas:	Why are they leaving?
Markel:	We've frightened them. They knew that we were going far away from here, and they left. They will never come back.

And so Marcel Proust escaped his melancholy, while returning to work on an important oeuvre that will not be seen before next year.

VERS BURLESQUES ET SATIRIQUES

BURLESQUES AND SATIRES

Vandal, exquis, répand son sel,
Mais qui s'en fout, c'est Gabriel,
Robert, Jean et même Marcel,
Pourtant si grave d'habitude.

46

A perfect Vandal has salt to spill
But who really cares, it's Gabriel,
Robert, Jean and even Marcel
Habitually so serious (and just as well).

47

Des gigolos mondains il est—dis-tu—le chef
Béatrice le goûte et Gustava l'invite
Parfois quittant Chaumeix, Jouvenel, Blum ou Vite
Vers Courance ou Verteuil va chasser Nonelef
Ainsi l'on voit parfois steamer esquif ou nef
Sans jamais se heurter à l'écueil qu'il évite
Voguer entre deux eaux qu'il dépassera vite
Y laissant son sillage éblouissant et net
Ainsi tu t'es trompé sur ce jeune poète
Il ne fréquente qu'un monde c'est son esprit.

47

You say he's the leader of wordly Gigolos.
Beatrice savors him and Gustava invites him to tea.
Sometimes departing Chaumeix, Jouvenel, Blum, or Vite
Off to Courance or Verteuil to chase Nonelef.
Just as sometimes we see a steamer, skiff, or ship,
Without ever striking the reef it skirts,
Drift carelessly over what it soon outsmarts
Leaving behind its dazzling clean wake.
And so you were wrong about this young poet.
He frequents only one world: his mind.

48

[. . .] n'a pas inventé
    La poudre
Sa femme est un Lancret renté,
    Sans poudre.
Une tache—disons, par réserve—de . . . thé
    Saupoudre
Sa jupe que bientôt, s'en va la vétusté
    Découdre
Et pourtant je la vois assez bien sous
    la berthe
De Thérésa, en organdi.
C'est pourquoi je préfère encore [. . .]
    J'ai dit.

48

[. . .] did not invent
       powder
His wife is a rented Lancret,
       Without powder.
A stain—we say, with reserve—of . . . tea
       Powdered
Her skirt quickly resuscitated
       Unstitched
And yet I saw it well under
       Theresa's
organdy bertha.
It's why I again prefer [. . .]
       I said.

49

CHANSON

Plus grosse que la baleine
            Et le narval
Est la bedaine, la bedaine
            De Bréval !
Malgré la sentence trop dure
            D'un chanteur rival
A son talent ma signature
            Donne l'aval.
Dieu quel passé de carnaval
Un tel amour à A.B. lègue :
Daudet, Lautier, Pol Neveu, Leygue,
Et le chaste auteur de Ferval.
L'amour même de Pierre Lalo
            Ô Mérétrice
Met à ton front comme un halo
            De Bérénice.

49

SONG

Bigger than the whale
  And the narwhal
Is the belly, the belly
  Of Bréval!
Despite a sentence too severe
  By a singing rival
For her talent my signature
  Rattles its rifle.
History! God what an eyeful.
Such love bequeathed to A.B.:
Daudet, Lautier, Pol Neveu, Leygue,
And the chaste author of Ferval.
The very love of Pierre Lalo
  O Meretrice
Makes your brow like a halo
  From Berenice.

Hélas quand ton triomphe, énorme, mondial,
Éclatant sur Salzbourg comme un feu boréal
      Issu près des Tropiques
Te jettera des fleurs autant qu'en vend Debac,
Et qu'au sein fulgurant des victoires épiques
T'acclameront Saint-Saëns et Gabriac !
Alors Ô Bunchnibuls, oublieux de Buncht même
Si, rival ténébreux de Losques et de Bac
Il envoie un dessin au Bunchnibuls qu'il aime
      Tu le jetteras au panier ?
      Ô Reynaldo peux-tu le nier ?
Hélas quand Rebecca murmurante et plaintive
Se redit, implorant le ciel pour qu'il survive,
      Les mots touchants d'Eléazar
Et, sublime inventeur, en sa grâce fortuite,
Ajoute à l'aria cette phrase inédite
      Que lui dicte le seul hasard !
Quand la Comtesse, hélas,—Isaac ou Farrar—
Profitant de l'instant où ne la voit personne
Caresse Chérubin que Beaumarchais soupçonne
      Et que divinise Mozart !
Que dans un bal vulgaire où, dans leur ressemblance,
Indistincts l'un de l'autre, d'Aramon s'élance
      Avec le Marquis Dadwisart
La chaleur les terrasse et leur fin serait proche
Si Griffon prévoyant ne sortait de sa poche
      L'extrait créé par Corvisart !
Quand Lilli voudrait bien ajouter—Ô Tessen !—
A son café mit milch des Delicatessen
      Dans quelque « Restauration »

Alas, when your triumph, broad as a palace,
Bursting over Salzburg like an aurora borealis
     Born near the Tropics
Tosses you enough flowers to clear out Debac,
And in the meteoric breast of victories epic
You're acclaimed by Saint-Saens and Gabriac—
Then, O Bunchnibuls, who his Buncht ignores,
If, tenebrous rival of Losques and Bac,
Buncht sends a sketch to the Bunchnibuls he adores
     Will you simply toss it away?
     O Reynaldo, can't you say?
Alas, when Rebecca, in plaintive moans,
Beseeching heaven for his safety, to herself intones
     The touching words of Eleazar
And, sublime inventor, in her fortuitous grace,
Adds to the aria this unheard phrase
     Prompted not by art!
When the Countess, alas—Isaac or Farrar—
Seizing the moment when no one sees,
Fondles Cherubino, bane of Beaumarchais
     And deity of Mozart!
And in a vulgar ball where, alike as gemini,
D'Aramon and the Marquis Dadwisart, his alibi,
Are nearly done in by the heat, were it not
For handy Griffon, who whips out on the spot
     The serum of Corvisart!
When Lili wishes to add—O Tessen!—
To her coffee mit milch a Delicatessen
     In some "Restauration"

Et pour cela bravant vingt fois Poséidon
Va courir—Ô rançon des femmes trop gourmandes—
Se cachant parmi les îles anglo-normandes.
Lorsque la Pourtalès vers qui Murat s'incline
Épuisera sur vous cette bouche câline
        Que désirèrent tant de rois
Et que sublime Iseult et moins illustre Alceste
L'illustre Félia voulant avoir son reste
        Prendra vos c . . . à la fois
Alors Ô ma beauté dites à la Litvinne
        Qui vous mangera de baisers
Que je garde l'essence et la forme divine
        De mes amours germanisés.

And so braving twenty Poseidons
Goes running off—O wages of female greed—
To hide in the Anglo-Norman islands.
When Pourtalès, before whom Murat bows,
Exhausts on you her teasing mouth
  That many a king misses
And vernacular Alcestis and Isolde sublime
The illustrious Felia desiring her part
  Takes your b . . . in both gloves
Then, O my beauty, tell that Litvinne tart
  Who devours you with kisses
That I keep the essence and form divine
  Of my Germanized loves.

Maure, balzacien, d'une marche pressée
Jean, lisse, avec des yeux ainsi qu'une pensée,
Lucien comme un caniche expressément tondu,
Douché, restant toujours désirable et dodu ;
Herrmann, par qui la Patience même est lassée,
Nijinski, de l'immense et sublime fusée,
Noirâtre, inconcevable et mince résidu ;
Bakhst spectre de la rose, âne de la carotte,
Boni, ventre de son, visage de poupée,
Sa main a toujours l'air de vous tendre une épée,
Son œil de vous juger et mettre à votre rang.

Moorish, complex as Balzac, quick on his feet,
Jean with the smooth complexion and the intense gaze;
Lucien, a meticulously sheared poodle,
Always well-scrubbed, plump and pretty;
Herrmann, who could wear down Patience herself;
Nijinski, sublime and explosive, a human rocket
Who soars across the stage, trailing smoke;
Bakhst, famed for staging the *Specter of the Rose,*
But also known as a randy donkey;
And Boni the dandy, a big doll of a man
With a pasty face and overstuffed belly,
Whose sword is always unsheathed, itching for a duel,
And whose stare can also cut you down to size.

Du silence des d'A . . .
Chacun ici-bas s'émerveille
Bertrand pourtant s'agite et veille
Et dit aux apaches : « Aimons ».

Sur les algues et goémons
Il lève un pêcheur solitaire
Et court par vaux et par monts
Mais il continue à se taire.

Tous unis devant ce mystère
Pauvres poètes nous rimons.
L'inconnu vers qui nous ramons
Guère plus que les d'A . . .
N'est taciturne et délétère.

Or que Bertrand soit blanc ou rouge
Les ouvriers parisiens
Que sa tendresse a fait siens
Au fond de l'alcôve et du bouge
Afin qu'il parle quelquefois
Depuis Juillet jusqu'en Décembre
Ont voulu lui donner leur voix
Et l'envoyer à la Chambre.

Car d'A . . . comme son père
Aime le pauvre prolétaire
Non dans son salon mais au lit
Et c'est tant mieux s'il le salit
D'un pied qui sent son militaire.

52

The silence of the D'A . . . on clan
Astonishes everyone and perplexes,
But Bertrand bustles and proposes
"love" to every hooligan.

From the seaweed and the sand
He plucked a quiet fisherman
And gallops over hill and dale
Keeping silent all the while.

Gathered before the Arcanum
We poets rhyme to beat the band,
Straining toward a great unknown
No more injurious or mum
Than the tribe of D'A . . . on.

Now whether Bertrand votes left or right
The Parisian working class
He's won with all his tenderness
In dingy bedrooms out of sight
Hoping he'll speechify for them
From July until December.
Let their voices swell for him
And thrust him back into the Chamber.

For D'A . . . just like his Dad
Loves the brawny, sweating prole
Not in his office, but in bed
And all the better if he'll soil
The sheets with stinking soldier's feet.

Il persuade l'enfant, il rajeunit le père
Au vieillard suppliant, il sait répondre « espère ».
Dans la main du potache il remet tout de gau
Ce trésor adoré que convoite Gourgaud
Et sur lequel Sala mit des lèvres dévotes
Et contre ses faveurs il demande des votes !
Au lascif apprenti qu'il tient si serré :
Si tu votes pour moi je recommencerai
Et [. . .] ton père et ton oncle et ton frère.
Tous le voudraient, il ne peut tous les satisfaire
Mais quand il est pressé il leur envoie son père
Et l'arrondissement pour sa gloire éclatante
Voulant un député se nomma une tante.

He entices the child, the father perks up,
To the supplicant geezer he promises hope.
In the hands of the schoolboy he places the treat
Gourgand's been lusting for and Sala's lips
Have moistened with his reverential sips.
And for all his favors, in return he wants votes!
To the randy shop-boy he fondles and pets:
"If you vote for me, I'll retool my rod
And F— your brother, your uncle and your Dad."
They're all panting for him, he can't keep up the pace,
But when he's busy he sends father in his place.
So the arrondissement, for its glory clear,
Needed a deputy, and voted in a queer.

53

On prétend qu'un russien, digne que Dieu le garde,
Sut éveiller encor un dernier sentiment
(En y laissant son corps glisser jusqu'à la garde)
Au cul pourtant tanné du pauvre Ferdinand.
  Que la flamme éparpille et arde
  Jusqu'à ma dernière harde
  J'évoquerais si j'étais barde
  Devant une foule hagarde
  L'inimaginable instrument
Plus dur en vérité qu'un métal de Dinant
Plus pressé qu'un foireux qui tarde
  Plus léger qu'un flocon qu'on carde
  Cinglant plus fort qu'une nasarde
  L'insensible paroi qu'il larde,
  Y virant comme une guimbarde,
  Tel le bateau lorsqu'il embarde
  Et le frôlant plus tendrement
  Que telle lèvre papelarde,
Le tout sans réveiller le moine Ferdinand.
Pourtant au sein d'un songe il crut qu'il sentait là
Le membre aimé jadis de . . . d'Antoine Sala
Ô souvenir exquis de la vingtième année
Il pressait d'un doigt lourd cette verge veinée
Que le sperme argentait comme un ruisseau d'avril
« Veux-tu que je t'enfile Antoine » , ainsi dit-il.
Répondit en chrétien le fils de Coralie :
Je ne veux qu'un échange, Ô toi (. . .)
Tu me (. . .) à l'Infante Elchie.

53

They say a Russian, may God preserve his soul,
Managed to rouse a flutter of sensation
In Ferdinand's leathery, tanned, and well-worked hole
By slipping in up to the hilt his brave baton.
     May fire consume to ash and coal
     My last rags and belongings all:
     If I were a poet, I would tell
     To a wide-eyed crowd the marvel
     Of this flabbergasting tool
Harder, I swear, than Dinant's well-forged iron,
Malingering like a coward from his battalion,
     Lighter than fluffy carded wool,
     Lashing that insensate wall
     It greases harshly with its drool,
     Swiveling there like an ancient wagon
     Or tilting like a heeling yawl
     And brushing it more tenderly than
     A touch from the lips of a cardinal.
All this without waking monkish Ferdinand.
Yet in dream he thought he was feeling—*ooh la la!*—
The once-beloved member of—Antoine Sala.
O exquisite memory of his twentieth year
When he pressed that veiny wand with heavy finger
And spurted out silver sperm like an April brook.
"Shall I screw you now, Antoine?" 'Twas thus he spoke.
To hear that good Christian, Coralie's son, reply:
"I want only one exchange, Ferdinand——i.e.:
that you——me to the Infanta Elchie."

Jeunes Filles en Fleurs

Laissons à Wagner l'ennuyeuse déesse Erde
Limon vil où Wotan se laissait oublier
Belle d'azur, pourtant quand vient un grain, la mer de
Marmara n'est que fange où périt maint voilier
S'il se laisse enliser, s'il a cargué trop tard
S'il n'a pas assez tôt supplié St. Médard,
Dont, tiré du latin, le vrai nom est St. Merde :
N'insistons pas, on doit savoir sacrifier
—Que l'étymologie elle-même se perde—
Les choses sans beauté, par exemple la merde.
Vous qui me couronnez jeunes filles en fleurs
Qu'habille le coutil, le satin ou la loutre,
Oubliez ces noirceurs ; préférez les couleurs
(Qu'évoque la méduse blanche aux reflets bleus)
Du seul nectar pour vous seules délicieux
Jeunes filles en fleurs, Ô buveuse de f . . .

54

BUDDING YOUNG GIRLS

Let Wagner keep Erda, that tiresome slit
Of foul silt who made Wotan forget the blue skies,
Even though any squall can turn the exquisite
Sea of Marmora into a mire that would capsize
Many sailboats, if let to sink or too late shortened sail,
If Saint Medardus was appeased, but to no avail,
Medardus, from *merda*, the Latin for Saint Shit:
But don't let's belabor it. For we should sacrifice
—What etymology itself can't admit—
Things without beauty, for example, shit.
You who crown me, dressed in rich sateens
Otter or tweed, budding young 'tweens
Forget brooding darks; prefer the prism
(It evokes the white jellyfish's ultramarine)
Of that singular nectar to you alone so pleasing
Budding young girls, O swallower of j . . .

POÈMES À . . .

POEMS TO . . .

55

À Reynaldo Hahn

Tu veux que ton basset soit misérable et souffre
Alors tu surgiras, tu l'arraches du gouffre
Et tu lui sembles Dieu !
Ô Reynaldo je suis ton basset lamentable
Qui ne peux te suivre comme un chien véritable
Et pleurera quand il devra te dire adieu

55

TO REYNALDO HAHN

You want your basset-hound to be miserable and suffering
So you can surge up and uproot him from the pit
And thus appear to him a God!
O Reynaldo I'm your lamentable basset-hound
Who can't tag along with you like a true dog
And who'll cry when he must bid you adieu

56

SUR LE TEMPS PLUVIEUX

Peut-être tu chéris moins que moi ces averses
Possible ! Les mentalités sont si diverses.

56

ON RAINY WEATHER

Perhaps you love, much less than me, these storms.
Could be. The mind will vary in its forms.

Le vieil hidalgo d'Este-Modène, ou de Parme
Qui nous voit à travers ton noble nez, Zadig
(Mieux qu'en le plus vivant Vélasquez de Madrid
Noir comme lui),—j'aime son charme
Et ses bonnes façons ; mais je verse une larme
Sur lui que j'eusse aimé ; et qui dit ton mystère
Brille de ce qui manque à ton parrain Voltaire.

57

The old nobleman of Este-Modena or Parma,
Who judges us by looking down *your* aristocratic nose,
  Zadig
(and sees us more clearly—sharing in his blackness—
like one of those vivid men Velasquez painted in Madrid).
I admire charm and fine manners,
But I shed a tear, too, knowing I would have loved the man
Who could unlock these mysteries with a brilliance
Your godfather Voltaire could not achieve.

Petit projet de gentil vitrail
Exécuté avec beaucoup troubail
À gauche on voit Marie et Félicie
Qui font lessive et disent quelle scie.
À droite Buninuls ne peut ouvrir poudre Legras
Et Binchdinuls vient pour alumser
Buninuls s'aide de genou et de bras
Binchdinuls est par colonne gothique en deux divisé
Tout ceci pour montrer à Binchdinuls quelque jour qu'il
fasse
Qu'il ne se passe pas jour sans que lui envoie petit
dessindicace.

58

Little project of sweet stained glass
To make it was a pain in the ass
On the left are Félicie and Marie
Who wash clothes and complain incessantly.
On the right Buninuls cannot open Legras powder
And Binchdinuls comes for alumsinum
Buninuls helps by knee and arms
Binchdinuls is divided by a gothic column
Everything here to show Binchdinuls what day it is
Not a day goes by without sending a little inscripartus.

59

Ni tenir une épée, un lys, une colombe,
Dans ma main que son corps tremblant [échappe] et
  bombe
Ne vaut tenir ta main, car le lys est moins pur
Et l'épée est moins noble.

59

Not holding a sword, a lily, a dove,
In my hand his body trembles (escaping) and swells
Not holding your hand, because the lily is less pure
And the sword is less noble.

60

Noël ! Noël !

Il est né l'enfant Reynaldo !
Sur le seuil « paved with emerald » (Ô . . .
Shakespeare !) les trois mages
Cyrille Paul et Wladimir
Viennent adorer tes ramages.

Il est né l'enfant Reynaldo !
      Noël ! Noël !

Où donc ai-je lu, Sainte Vierge !
Dans l'*Imparcial*, le *Heraldo*
Où fit ses débuts Daniel Vierge
Qu'espagnol était Reynaldo
Espagnol né dans son dodo

L'enfant amour, l'enfant divin, Ô Sainte Vierge !
Là le fait est prouvé je veux t'offrir un cierge.

60

NOEL! NOEL!

He is born the child Reynaldo!
On the threshold "paved with emerald" (O . . .
Shakespeare!) the three wise men
Cyrille Paul and Wladimir
Come, as you sing, to adore
You, born! the child Reynaldo!
      Noel! Noel!

Where then did I read, Holy Virgin
In the *Imparcial* or in the *Heraldo*
Where Daniel Vierge got his start
That Spanish was Reynaldo
Spanish born in his heart

Love's child, divine child, O Holy Mother,
Here proved by the fact that I light you a candle.

En remerciement d'une réponse admirable

Qui n'écrirait sans cesse afin d'un jour te lire !
Le soleil monstrueux palpite dans ta lyre,
Quand tu daignes chanter, Mozart dit « Taisons-nous »
Et l'on peut voir alors les peuples à genoux
D'où monte, effusion des sublimes ondées
Le flot prodigieux des strophes débordées.
Alors de rage on voit Weber briser son luth,
L'amateur vient siffler ce qui jadis lui plut,
César Franck et Fauré n'ont qu'à fermer boutique,
Offenbach redemande un peu de sel attique
Et voit avec stupeur lui rire au nez Vénus.
Et partout t'implorant de leurs deux bras, venus
Les uns de Delphes où Phoebus, ce dieu t'aime !
Cabrant ses étalons sur un rythme suprême
Sème la graine d'or que seul tu recueillis,
Les autres de la côte où foisonnent les lys,
Et tous ceux de Mégare et ceux de Acrocorinthe
Où l'enfant d'Ictinos rit encor sur la plinthe,
Ceux d'Argos l'hippiaque et ceux de Ctésiphon,
Ceux qui sur la mer glauque et mugissante font
Le sol natal plus grand des îles asservies
Venaient te faire don de leurs âmes ravies.
Car telle est la vertu de ton chant Reynaldo
Il te suffit de ré mi fa sol la si do
Des sept sons de la flûte aux tiges inégales
Pour asservir d'un chant plus doux que les cigales
        Adorable :
Sparte avec ses héros, l'Olympe avec ses dieux.

In Gratitude for Such an Admirable Reply

I'd never stop writing you back, hoping once more to read
  your desire!
The prodigious sun pulsates in your lyre,
When you deign to sing, Mozart tells us "Quiet please"
And then all the people fall to their knees
From which arises an effusion of showers sublime
A prodigious flood of outpouring rhyme.
Then we see Weber break his lute out of rage,
The amateur boos what once used to engage,
Cesar Franck and Fauré might as well close up shop,
And Offenbach demand a little more Attic salt
Then see him laugh giddily right in Venus's face.
And yet, from Delphi they have come to embrace
you with outstretched arms, because Phoebus loves you!
His sun stallions rear up at your supreme tune
Scattering golden seed right into your spoon,
Those from the coast where the lilies abound,
And all those from Megara and from Acrocorinth
Where the child of Ictinus still laughs on his plinth,
Those from equestrian Argos and from Ctesiphon,
Those that, of all the islands enthralled upon
The lowing murky sea, hail from the largest homeland did
Come to offer you their souls all enchanted.
Because such is the quality of your singing, Reynaldo,
That it is enough for you to re mi fa sol la ti do
The seven sounds of the uneven pan flute
To enthrall with a voice softer than that of cicadas
        Adorable:
Sparta with its heros, Olympus with its gods.

62

L'infini raisonneur dit à Kant : entends-tu ?
L'impératif finit à ce turlututu
Car l'aigle liberté s'échappe du nid cause
À ton texte de l'art ajoute cette glose
Et mets Sorel avant Monteverde et Wagner.

62

The infinite reasoner says to Kant: Do you hear?
The imperative ends with a flourish of cornets,
And Freedom, like an eagle, flees the nest of causality.
Consider art accordingly in all your works—
Elevate Sorel above Monteverdi and Wagner.

Ô Reynaldo je te dirai lansgage !
Puisque à dessein tu partis—insensé !
Dans le moment que prenant mon courage
À deux mains, et d'un pas pressé
Du *Figaro* j'ouvris l'ultime page
Ô Reynaldo je te dirai lansgage !
Mais mon enfant souffre que ma sagesse
S'inspire ici des dictons anciens
Ne craignant pas de les faire siens.
Ainsi Racine en use avec la Grèce
Et Moréas . . . Pardon ! Ô lyre enchanteresse
Ô toi qui charmas Gustava et sa détresse
Pardonne-moi divin musicien
Ô successeur d'Ange Politien.
Pourquoi, te diras-tu, Marcel veut-il m'écrire ?
Minuit est dépassé, sa couche le rapelle.
Mais ton pigeon sent battre encor son aile
Et veut courir jusqu'à ton oreiller
Sa tendresse pour toi Ô Buninuls est telle
Que, pensant à Salzbourg elle le fait veiller
Mais le sommeil aussi le fait déjà bâiller,
Rothschild est un banquier, dit-on, plein de mérite
Déposer son argent chez lui est le cher rite
De tout ce qui possède, Espagne ou Mexicain.
Aussi donc au cocher, sans peur dis : rue Laffitte !
Robert y veille aussi, beau comme une Charite,
Sur le seuil du logis la Fortune est écrite
Tant de gens ont monté ce degré qui s'effrite
Que cet ancien logis tenterait Henri Cain.

63

Reynaldo, hear, I shall thee now address!
Since off you went, on purpose, crazy child!—
Just at the moment when, in spite of stress
And plucking up my courage to be bold,
I turned to the *Figaro*'s last pages, flipping fast—
Reynaldo, hear, I shall thee now address.
Patience, my boy, and suffer that my art
Should draw its strength from ancient practices
Not fearing to take them to its modern heart.
This is the way Racine used Ancient Greece
And Moréas . . . Forgive me! Magic lyre,
O you who charmed Gustava in her distress,
Divine musician, Poliziano's heir.
And why, you'll say, does Marcel write to me?
It's past midnight, his bed is beckoning,
But your pet pigeon flutters still his wing
And wants to speed to your pillow straightaway.
His love for you, O Buninuls, runs so deep
That thinking of Salbourg keeps him from his sleep
Though sheer exhaustion forces him to yawn.
Rothschild's an excellent banker, so they say,
And everyone who's got some cash to play
Goes straight to him from Mexico or Spain.
So tell the driver, Hurry! Rue Lafitte!
Robert keeps watch there too, a dazzling sight.
Upon the threshold, Fortune itself is writ.
So many have climbed those stairs, now wearing down,
That the old mansion would tempt even Henri Cain.
And who cares a fig if Drumont throws a fit?

Et qu'importe
après tout si Drumont s'en irrite ?
Qui s'en va chez Lecoffre acheter son bouquin ?
Mais Buncht, Ô mon enfant, veille à ton patrimoine !
Le régime actuel a beau manger du moine,
Alarmer follement nos plus chers intérêts,
Il est encor, crois-moi, des placements prospères,
On insulte l'armée, on expulse les Pères,
Mais la rente remonte aussi quand tu parais
Poincaré ! Donc Ô Buncht, spécule, agiote, espère !
Cela vaut bien autant que d'être militaire.
Et s'il fut autrefois dieu des filous sur terre
Hermès, ne dis pas non ! vaut cependant Arès.
Tu diras qu'une bourse aussitôt qu'elle sonne
Charme ; mais vide hélas, il n'y a plus personne
Ainsi que dit la Marquise d'Albufera.
Mais ne sois pas enfant, Ô Reynaldo raisonne !
Écoute Robert de Rothschild (je le soupçonne !)
Il te dira mon cher ce que faire il faudra.
Peut-être la Russie autrefois richissime
Étant si bas, te dira-t-il de t'y lancer
Comme un désespéré parvenu sur la cime
Qui veut tenter un soir l'infini de l'abîme
À mon très humble avis ce serait plus qu'un crime
Le tsar est un enfant et l'Ukaz—Potemkine,
Prouve que le Commerce ira, sans se laisser
Arrêter par Guillaume ou le Maréchal Prime,
D'ailleurs le trois pour cent ne fait déjà plus prime.
Je ne te le dis pas, crois-moi, « quant à » la rime
Ce sont jeux auxquels je ne daigne me baisser
Et la preuve c'est que je m'en vais me cousser
Sans même demander mon cher à t'embrascher.
                    Bonjours

Who goes to Lecoffre to buy his silly book?
But Buncht, my child, guard your inheritance!
Though this regime is roughing up the monks
And putting good society in shock,
Believe me, it's still safe to purchase stock.
They spit on the Army, they expel the priests,
But the market soars when you appear, O Poincaré.
So, dear Buncht, hope, speculate, invest!
It's just as noble as the Army life
And if Hermès is god of swindlers on the earth,
So be it.—Even though Ares has his day.
You'll say a full purse, clinking, brings good cheer
And friends; when it's empty, lo, they disappear
As the Marquise of Albufera has wisely said.
But don't be a child, Reynaldo, use your head!
Listen to Robert de Rothschild (though he's sly):
He'll tell you exactly what you ought to buy.
Maybe Russia, once so rich and now so low,
Is where you ought to hurl your money now
Like a mountaineer who scales the peak and sighs
And, desperate, wants to plunge to the abyss.
In my humble view, that move would be a crime:
The Tsar's a kid, and his decree a sham.
Business marches on, in spite of William
And the machinations of Maréchal Prime.
In any case, three percent's no longer premium.
Don't listen to me, I'm prattling. As for rhyme,
Those are games I don't even deign to play.
And for proof, just look: I'm going beddie-bye
Without even asking, Toots, to kiss you Nightie-nigh.
                    Good morning!

64

De tourner la fenêtre, de dépister l'issue
Et de pénétrer dans l'appartement,
Notre maître matou vous le pensez bien
N'en eut que pour un moment.

(Lafontaine hasrangé)

64

Turn from the window, lose the way out
And enter the apartment,
Our old master you will understand
Wasn't there but for an instant.

(LAFONTAINE DERANGED)

Chanteur, pardonne-moi d'ici te déranger.
   Ô Dieux ! —Ô Muses ! —
Je sais qu'en t'affrontant je risque le danger
   De Pelénor et d'Ellébuse !
Si Léon n'intercède, je subirai le sort
   Hélas d'Orphée
Sans compter les parfums qu'épand ta tête d'or
   Lorsque tu l'as coiffée !
Peut-être en ce moment tu sens tous les onguents
   Qu'on ne peut nier sans mentir,
Et, satisfait de toi, tu réclames tes gants,
   D'Auguste, pour sortir !
Sur ton cheveu tu mets encor de l'hypocras
   Et marches vers la porte
Je demande un seul mot, mais à toi que t'importe
   Si t'attend Moréas !
Autrefois tu connus pourtant plus d'un aède
   Épris du vaste éther !
Saint Ygest qui chanta le Cygne et Ganymède
   Fernand Gregh et Peter.
Mais le disciple est loin des dieux dont il émane
   Labori n'est point Hild
Et point encor n'atteint à Jean de Castellane
   Robert—Louikke—de Rothschild
Et pourtant d'une voix pète—sèche et mielleuse
   J'ose te déranger !
Accorde-moi cette chose délicieuse :
   L'adresse de Nordlinger.

65

Crooner, pardon if I interrupt anything important
      O Gods!—O Muses!—
I know that in confronting you I risk the misfortune
      Of Peleanor and Ellébeuse!
And if Leon does not intervene, I will suffer the fate
      Of Orpheus—Alack!
Not to mention the fragrance that wafts off your pate
      Whenever it's freshly slicked back!
Perhaps in this instance, made more than usually smug
      by the pomade's smell suffusing
you call to Auguste to "bring your gloves"
      with thoughts of going cruising
You smear your hair with a little more mousse
      And walk confidently toward the door
Though I am asking a brief word and no more
      if you're to meet Moréas, what's the use!
And yet, there was a time when you knew more than one
      bard in love with the boundless ether!
Saint Ygest, who sang of Ganymede and the Swan
      Fernand Gregh, and Peter.
Yet the disciple is far from his original afflatus—
      Labori is no Hild it's plain—
And Robert de Rothschild can't reach the status
      Of Jean de Castellane.
And yet in a curt and honeyed voice I'm daring
      to interrupt you nevertheless!
Grant me this one delicious thing
      Marie Nordlinger's address!

Mais non, Reboux l'emporte et la faveur du Buncht
L'intronise en un rang qui n'était dû qu'à Guncht !
Bardac ne déplait point, Ochsé règne, Straram
Peut dire en me voyant hélas : « He was, I am »
Léon visite seul cet ami qu'on délaisse.
Ce poney qui souvent tend nez pour que caresse . . .

66

But no, Reboux takes it up and the favor of Buncht
Enthrones him on a rung meant only for Guncht.
Bardac is not a bust, Ochsé rules, Straram
Seeing me can say, alas, "He was, I am"
Léon alone visits this friend they leave out.
This pony, seeking pets, oft puts forth his snout.

67

Plutôt qu'à ce rêveur, cet amoureux d'abeilles (1)
Que ne réclamais-tu le doux fruit de mes veilles (2)
Ô toi qui connais mieux la Vierge d'Avila,
Reynaldo Hahn ! ! que . . . que . . . que le lait Mamila !
Je t'embrasse (3) pourtant musicien volage (4)
Qui change si souvent de barbe et de pelage.

Hasdieu Gruncht.

Notes du commentateur dans un siècle.
(1) Sans doute, d'abeilles d'Hymette, au figuré : un poète.
(Non, marteau, c'est Maeterlinck.)
(2) Au figuré : mes œuvres. Car à en juger par le petit
nombre d'ouvrages qu'il a laissé, il ne paraît pas probable
que M. Proust se couchait tard.
(3) Figuré
(4) Figuré : inconstant

67

More so than for this dreamer, this lover of bees (1)
That you rejected the sweet fruit of my nights without
    sleep (2)
O you who know the Virgin of Avila,
Reynaldo Hahn!! better than . . . than . . . than the milk of
    Mamilla!
I embrace you (3) though you're an inconstant musician (4)
And change your beard and your fur so often.

    Hasdieu Gruncht

Notes of the commentator a century later.
(1) Without a doubt, the bees of Hymette, figure for: a
poet. (No, numbskull, it's Maeterlinck.)
(2) Figure for: my works. For, judging from the small
number of works he has left, it does not seem likely that
M. Proust went to bed late.
(3) Figured
(4) Figured: inconstant

Hélas seul de tant d'illustres
    Ducs et rustres
Pour Chicago et Boston
Seul, ne peut t'offrir, Ô maistre !
    Une lettre,
L'ermite Porte-Bâton
Dettellbach ou Chevigné
    —Résigné—
Aux Yankees te recommande
    Et leur mande
De prendre comme leçon
    Ta chanson.
Wladimir noble grand duc
    —bien caduc ! —
Adresse de son pupitre
    Mainte épître
Non pas—à quoi bon ? —aux Fould,
    Mais aux Gould !
La Pourtalès débonnaire
Dont sera le centenaire
Cet an—trop tard—célébré,
De sa plume originale
    Te signale
Au consul Alcide Ebray !
Tous ceux à qui ta Chronique
    Fait la nique
Jusqu'aux Reskés de Noufflard
Font s'élever tes louanges
    Jusqu'aux anges
Pour tous ces marchands de lard.

68

Alas, only one of so many illustrious
   Dukes and boors
From Chicago and Boston
One alone, is able to offer you, O maestro!
   A letter,
The reclusive Baton-Holder
Dettellbach or Chevigné
   —Resigned—
recommends you to the Yankees
   And directs them
To learn a lesson from
   Your song.
Noble Grand Duke Vladimir
   —well wasted!—
Pontificates from his lectern
   Many an epistle
Not—and for what?—to the Foulds
   But to the Goulds!
The debonair Comtesse Pourtalès
who will feted this year—too
late—a centenarian
In her singular writing
   Singles you out
To Alcide Ebray the consul!
All those at whom your review
   Cocks a snook
Even Noufflard's Reskés
Sing your praises
   To the skies
For all these purveyors of bacon.

Air du Pont des Soupirs

Un jour l'ermite de Versailles
Écrivit à son Reynaldo :
Comme je suis sans sou ni mailles a, ailles
Ah ! ne crois pas à un Kasdeau
Ah ! Ah ! Ah ! Ah ! Ah ! Ah !

C'est une action de tramway électrique
Que pour toi j'ai su bien placer,
Et tu ne vas pas, je m'en pique,
Me refuser. Refuser !
Ah ! Ah ! Ah ! Ah ! Ah ! Ah !

Cette affaire où ma science unique
A bien su pour toi spéculer
                    (*avec force*)
C'est le tramway électrique
Je vais, je vais te l'envoyer !
Ah ! Ah ! Ah ! Ah ! Ah ! Ah !

69

SONG OF THE BRIDGE OF SIGHS

One day the hermit of Versailles
Wrote to his Reynaldo:
I'm without a cent or a stitch—sigh, sigh—
Ah! don't believe in a "gift"
Ah! Ah! Ah! Ah! Ah! Ah!

Electric tramway stock
For your sake I knew to buy
And you won't, I'm proud to say,
Refuse me. Refuse!
Ah! Ah! Ah! Ah! Ah! Ah!

That business where my unique sapience
Knew how, for your sake, to speculate
                    (*with force*)
Get set for the electric tram
I'm gonna send to you!
Ah! Ah! Ah! Ah! Ah! Ah!

Tandis qu'assis dans un bac
Fleuri d'œillets de Debac
[Sur l'onde] je suis Esbac
L'auteur préféré de Schwabach
Sur les rives du Potomac
Cher éléphant de Dramouak
Admirateur de Sulbac
Plusque de Bretagneche et Carnac
Et de Gustava née Anspach
Tu vas retrouver ton cornac
D'Oxford, le jeune Bardac
Qui ne vint point chez Polignac
Qui pour toi a remplacé Bach
Et ma montre qui fait tic tac
Accroît à chaque instant mon trac
Que pris dans le triste ressac
De tout cet ennuyeux mic-mac
Tu ne viennes pas Ô cher crac !
Prends donc ton clic et ton clac
Accours, car j'ai dans mon sac
Un mot nouveau de Fézensac
Sur Laszlo, ce second Lenbach.

70

While sitting on a ferry taking stock
Blooming with carnations from Debac
[On the waves] I am Esbac
The favorite author of Schwabach
On the banks of the Potomac
Dear Elephant Dramouak
Admirer of Sulbac
More than Bretagneche and Carnac
And Gustava born Anspach
Your mahout's parked out back
From Oxford, the young Bardac
Who did not visit Polignac
Who for you replaced Bach
And my watch that tick-tocks
Constantly increases my tracks
Caught in the sad surf's wracks
Of all this intrigue, dull and black
You're not coming O dear crack!
So take your click and your clack
Hasten, for I have in my sack
The latest word from Fezensac
About Lazlo, this second Lenbach.

SONNET

Collabore avec Louis le Gendre
Ou même avec Hugues Delorme,
Et pendant ce temps laisse attendre
Ton poney,—Ô moschant ! —sous l'orme ;

À Vaudoyer montre un cœur tendre
Et, que Larguier excelle ou dorme,
Déclare son talent énorme
À Reboux qui te sait entendre ;

Voici le livre curieux
Du « bon poète » des Rieux
Que ton pauvre moschant t'ensvoie.

C'est avec bien chasgrin au cœur
Qu'il délaisse aux autres la joie
D'être ton collaborateur.

SONNET

With Louis Le Gendre collaborate
Or even Hugues Delorme you can
And meanwhile let your pony wait
Under the elm, you nefasty man!

To Vaudoyer show a tender heart
And, that Larguier excels or bores us,
Declare his talents enormous
To Reboux, who always attends your part.

Here's that peculiar little tome
Of that "good poet" des Rieux's pome
That your nefasty man sends you.

It's with a heart so sadly and sore
That he cedes to others the joy
Of being your collaborator.

72

Ô toi que m'as mené chez la de Castellane
Ô Buncht, Ô Reynaldo !
Et qui jadis ornas la prose mosellane
De Barrès avec tes mi fa sol la si do.

Toi qui voles d'un bond de l'hysope à la cime
Mesures Léonard dans toute sa hauteur
Puis sans trouver après, Ô découvreur sublime
De l'esprit à Rosa Malheur !

Toi qui quand tu le veux sais replier tes ailes
Être gourmand et roupillard
Et plus divin encore multiplier tes zèles
Chez Risler et chez Hopillard !

Toi qui aux mécréants dis *Venise la Rouge*
En les invectivant
Ou reviens chez ton Buncht après le concert Rouge
Plus vite que le vent !

Écoute Ô Reynaldo d'autres aiment la gloire
L'Institut, la Raunay
Mais moi cher Reynaldo, (je veux que tu me croire)
Je n'ai que mon Poney.

72

O you who have brought me to de Castellane's home
O Buncht, O Reynaldo!
And who used to embellish the Mosellean prose
Of Maurice Barrès with your mi fa sol la ti do.

You who can fly in one leap from the hyssop to the peak
And stand as tall as Leonardo in all his height
Yet still cannot, O sublime adventurer, discover
Intelligence in Rosa Malheur!

You who, when you want to, can fold up your wings,
And become a gourmand and good sleeper
And more divine still, add to your enthusiasms
      Chez Hopillard and Risler!

You who, when insulting miscreants,
      Recite "Venise la Rouge"
Or after the *Rouge* performance return chez your Buncht
      Faster than any luge!

Listen, O Reynaldo, others love fame
The *Institut de France* and Jeanne Raunay
But me, dear Reynaldo, (I want you to believe me)
I have only my Pony.

À Wafflard, Brack ou Collardeau
Que peut préférer Reynaldo ?
Sur ce point ma sentence hésite
Mais ce n'est pas, disons-le vite,
Certes, la Symphonie en do !

Quel peut bien être son credo ?
Est-ce celui du bedeau ?
Est-ce celui du lévite ?
Mais ce n'est pas, disons-le vite,
Certes, la Symphonie en do !

Le Dimanche, près du Rideau
Qu'aime-t-il entendre : Brindeau
Kolb, la Tosca, la Carmélite ?
Mais s'il se hâte et s'il évite
D'Albu, Modène et Camondo
Ce n'est pas pour ouïr plus vite
Certes, la Symphonie en do.

Avant d'aller faire dodo
Que va-t-il entendre, Nado ?
Serait-ce à l'Eldorado
Fragson que lui-même imite
Ou Féraudy dans du Sandeau ?
Mais non pas disons-le bien vite
Certes, la Symphonie en do.

73

Of Wafflard, Brack or Collardeau
Who's your preference, Reynaldo?
At this point all my thoughts run slow
But I have to say, without demur,
Not the Symphony in C, for sure!

Which credo does he now embrace?
Comes it from a bedel's place?
Comes it from the Levite race?
But I have to say, without demur,
Not the Symphony in C, for sure!

Sunday, he's next to the curtain
What would he like to hear: Brindeau,
Kolb, Tosca, or the Carmelite?
If he rushes off and steers clear
Of Modène, Camando, and d'Albu
It's not so he can sooner hear
The Symphony in C, that's for sure.

Before he's off to beddy-byes
What would he hear, Nado?
Would it be in the El Dorado
Fragson, who's himself, in his guise
Or Féraudy in a Sandeau piece?
I have to say, there's no allure,
Not the Symphony in C, for sure.

Si je veux lui faire Kasdeau
Que donnerais-je à Reynaldo
Des najares, un fricandeau
Ou des chants de la Sulamite
Mais non pas Ô disons-le vite
Certes la Symphonie en do.

If I'm giving him a "Geeft"
What's the thing for Reynaldo?
Tangerines, a fricando,
The songs of *La Sulamite*?
But no, O, say it, without demur,
No Symphony in C, for sure.

74

Quatrains pour Guninuls

J'ai vu Picquart mentir aux Ménard d'Orian,
D'Arnoux paraître fin aux foules d'Orient,
Alvarez faire un Kouac qu'il esquive en riant
Mais vîtes-vous, Ô Joseph, Ô Reginald, Ô
Wladimir, d'un bémol se tromper Reynaldo ?

Leclerc connaît à fond le théâtre de Lope
De Vega ; parisien pourtant il goûte Ibels
Mais à ce que prétend un mensteur (Funibels)
Il n'aurait jamais entendu parler de Pénélope.

74

QUATRAINS FOR GUNINULS

I saw Picquart lie to Ménard Dorian,
D'Arnoux appear refined to crowds of the Orient,
Alvarez hit the wrong note when he ducked with a laugh
But do you see how, O Joseph, O Reginald, O
Wladimir, that one flat note upset Reynaldo?

Leclerc knows the depths of the theater of Lope
De Vega; although Parisian he has a taste for Ibels
But for the claims of a fibster (Funibels)
He would never have heard of Penelope.

75

J'étais seul, j'attendais auprès de la fenêtre.
C'était il m'en souvient par une nuit d'automne,
Ou plutôt Buninuls c'était cette nuit-ci
Le murmure du vent de son bruit monotone
Dans mon esprit lassé berçait de noirs soucis.

75

I was alone, I waited close to the window.
It was I remember on an autumn night,
Or rather Buninuls it was that night
The murmur of the wind of his monotonous sound
In my tired spirit dark thoughts abound.

Abords du Palais (partie opposée de l'île)
Où gîte maintenant mon petit Reynaldo,
Roi,—seul Roi—, du do, ré, mi, fa, sol, la, si, do
Et qui ne pense pas à son petit poulain
Tandis que celui-ci lui fait ce joli dessin.

76

About the Palace (the opposite side of the island)
Now where nestles my little Reynaldo,
King,—sole King—, of do, re, me fa, sol, la, ti, do
And who doesn't think about his little pony
Even though he draws him a picture so pretty.

Plutôt que d'aimer un meschant
    Contre toute espérance

Que fier, et sans raison, de son art et son chant
    Ne répond pas à ma souffrance !
Et sur les flots d'azur où mainte voile cargue
    Voit venir mes dessins,
Mais lui ne répond pas, en fait fi, et me nargue
    À dessein !

Sur le roc arc-bouté comme dans une église
    Il regarde juser
Le flot décomposé qui bout et s'opalise
    Et l'écoute jaser ;
Dans la grotte il descend quoique n'étant pas brave,
    Hasarde un pied mal sûr,

Et voit sur les cristaux le flot secret qui bave
    Des améthystes et de l'azur ;
Puis du fond des palais il remonte en fringale
    Car il a toujours faim
Et dans son cher palais qu'il prétend avoir fui
La nourriture poissonneuse ou végétale
    Se succède sans fin !

Alors, Sarah, Clarisse, s'exclament « Ô mon maître
    Que vas tu nous chanter ? »
Mais lui répond « ne pourrions-nous bientôt nous mettre
    à diner ? »

77

Rather than loving someone wrong
    Against all hoping

Who proud, with no reason, of his art and his song
    Doesn't answer my moping!
And, on the azure waves where many a sail breezes
    Foresees my sketch,
But doesn't answer, ignores it, and teases
    Me, the wretch!

On the rock arched as in a church
    He sees the tide sinking
The waves decomposed turning opal in the lurch
    And listen to him talking
Descending in the grotto though no brave fool
    He risks a foot unsure,

Seeing on the crystals the secret waves drool
    Amethysts and azure;
Then he rises from the palace depths peckish
    For he is always hungry

And in his dear palace he pretends to have fled
    Whether the food be vegetables or fish
    It abounds infinitely!

Then Sarah and Clarissa, exclaim "Oh my master
    What will you sing to us?"
But he responds "Couldn't we dine with no fuss?"

Puis il descend au port, accoudé sur la môle
    Ne pense point Marcelche,
Mais se dit : je pourrais aller voir à la Baule
    Risler aux yeux de Welsche.

Il revoit le palais Sanzon mais n'a point cure
    Des souvenirs défunts
Ne donne nul penser à l'autre Dioscure
Qui n'aime pas trop les parfums.
    Assez.

Then he goes down to the port, leans on a pier
      Doesn't think of Marcelche
But says to himself: in La Baule I could peer
      At Risler with the eyes of Welche.

He sees again the Sanzon palace but cares not
      For the memories now bygone
Gives another Dioscuros not the slightest thought
Who doesn't like perfumes on,
      Enough.

78

À Robert de Billy

Ton esprit, divin chrysanthème,
Douloureux avec majesté,
Un jour nous redira les thèmes
De la douleur de la beauté.

78

To Robert de Billy

Your spirit, divine chrysanthemum,
Aching with majesty,
One day will reprise for us the prose
Of beauty's intrinsic suffering.

Chanson sur Robert

Droit comme un piquet, sec comme une pierre,
    Où qu'est son charme ?
On n'aura jamais, sous sa paupière,
    Même une larme.

Ô pierre à fusil, droite route grise,
    Où qu'est ses charmes ?
Ô route ou caillou—qu'avez-vous qui grise,
    Chose sans larmes ?

    Pourtant il est des pays
    Uniformes, secs et gris
    Que d'aucuns trouvent jolis.

    Ils croient que leur ciel fâché
    Révèle un Dieu, une âme
    Que ne trahit nulle flamme.
    C'est un Dieu bien caché.
M. X . . . eût dit dans sans langue immortelle :
« Ce ciel recèle Dieu, plus qu'il ne le révèle. »
Vous recèlez un Dieu, Robert, entendez-vous ?
    Et ce n'est pas moi qui l'ai dit,
    Mais un ivrogne sans esprit.
Vous recèlez un Dieu, Ô route de cailloux
Bien droite, sous un ciel uniforme et fâché.
Moi je chemine avec, en mon cœur, l'espoir doux
    Qu'un Dieu dans ce ciel est caché.

79

SONG ON ROBERT

Uptight as a picket, dry as a boy's rock,
     What's his appeal?
Never a thing, beneath his lid,
     Not even a tear.

O silex, gunshot-straight gray road,
     Where are his charms?
O road or pebble—how come you intoxicate,
     Thingamabob without tears?

     Nevertheless there are countries
     Uniform, dry and gray
     That some folks find pretty.

     They believe that their pissed-off sky
     Reveals a God, a soul
     Betraying no flame.
     That's a God well-hid.
Mr. X has said in his immortal tongue:
"That sky conceals God more than it reveals."
You harbor a God, Robert, did you hear?
     And I'm not the one who said it—
     Just some drunkard without spirit.
You hide a God, O pebbly road
Right straight, under a sky uniform and pissed-off.
Me, I trudge with—in my heart—a sweet hope
     That a God in the sky lies hid.

80

À MADELEINE LEMAIRE

Quel trop subtil voleur coupa dans les vergers
Ces raisins lumineux dont ma lèvre est éprise ?
Le zéphyr souffla ces chandelles par surprise
Lui seul est assez doux pour ne les pas blesser.

Main non, pour les pinceaux quittant fuseaux et laine
Vous faites plus que Dieu : un éternel printemps,
Et c'est auprès des lys et des rosiers grimpants
Que vous allez chercher vos couleurs, Madeleine.

Vous avez la beauté frêle de l'éphémère,
Et pourtant fleurs d'un jour vous ne périrez pas,
Fleurs vivant et pourtant immortelles : lilas,
Œillets ou lys qu'a peints Madeleine Lemaire.

Mais vous, qui vous peindra, belle jardinière
Par qui tous les printemps nous naissent tant de fleurs ?

80

For Madeleine Lemaire

Which surreptitious thief clipped from this orchard
These luminous grapes that so delight my lips?
The zephyr blows the candle's flames about
He alone is soft enough not to snuff them out.

Disdaining wool and spindles for the brush
You outpace God: a springtime without end;
And from the lily and the climbing rose
You orchestrate your palette, Madeleine.

Your beauty is as fleeting as the mayfly
Yet, flowers of one day, you shall not fade.
Living flowers and yet immortal: lilacs,
Carnations, or lilies that Miss Lemaire has made.

But whoever shall paint you, gardener fair,
Who each spring conjure flowers from thin air?

81

Au Convive

Ami, cherche la fraise entre les violettes.
Vois les fleurs ont couvert la table de leur reine
Et mêlent, liserons muguets ou bien aigrettes,
Leur doux charme au charme plus doux de Madeleine.

Ne crains rien, les méchants n'oseront t'y chercher
Notre hôtesse est vaillante aussi bien qu'elle est tendre
Elle a des douceurs pour t'aimer
Mais des griffes pour te défendre.

Ici, comme le vin, l'esprit est délectable
Les fleurs qui couronnaient les fronts, ceignent la table
Pour une qu'elle eut peinte on donnerait leur plaine
Vois, quel bonheur ! Le sourire de Madeleine.

81

To the Guest

Friend, seek the strawberry amid the violets,
See, the flowers have covered the queen's table then
And mix, bindweed, lilies, or else aigrettes,
Their sweet charm sweeter still of Madeleine.

Fear not, the wicked there won't dare to seek you
Our hostess is valiant as well as tender
  She has sweetness to love you
  But claws to be your defender.

Here, just like wine, the mind is delectable
Flowers that graced foreheads now gird the table
For the one she'd have painted you'd give your last mile
See, what joy! It's Madeleine's smile.

À Marie Nordlinger

Ta main qui, comme l'eau, reflète les nuages
    De ton esprit
    Et ses images ;
Et, comme le flot, rythme, avec ses belles
    rages
La matière qu'en ses doigts puissants elle prit,
Entre ses doigts puissants et sages ; —
À quel beau rameau d'or, mystérieuse Hébé,
A-t-elle, pour un don magique, dérobé
Le nectar purpurin d'un quadruple élytre ?
À travers la divine et translucide vitre
Je vois auprès de l'émeraude l'améthyste
Qui fera, si tu veux, que mon cœur soit moins
    triste !
Autour des ballons blancs du fruit délicieux
C'est le quadruple sort qui sait fléchir les cieux !
Et l'émail à qui tu fais tout dire Ô Marie,
Soit que le beau coq chante ou que le verger rie
Dans le plat merveilleux où je crois voir encor
L'émail marin qu'enclôt le pâle cuivre d'or !
Sur les flots interdits fais palpiter ta rame !
La matière est fermée : entrouvre-la, Sésame !
Et de tes mains, toujours plus nobles et sereines
Sur les trésors des Rois plante les lys des
    Reines !
À tes goûts préférés je veux joindre les miens
Enchâsse les beautés de Chartres et d'Amiens
Dans le cuivre docile ou dans l'émail rebelle.

82

FOR MARIE NORDLINGER

Your hand, like water, reflects the clouds
     Of your spirit
     And its images;
And, like the tide, rhythm, with its beautiful rages
The substance she took up with her strong fingers,
—Between her strong and wise fingers;—
From which golden bough did mysterious Hebe
Steal the purple nectar of the fourfold wing
For a magic gift?
Through the divine and translucent glass
Near the emerald amethyst I see
What will make, if only you give the word, my heart less sad!
Around the luscious fruit's white balls
This is the fourfold fate that knows how to bend the skies!
Touch the heavens
And the enamel you fashion so it expresses everything, O
    Marie,
So that the handsome rooster crows, or that the orchard
    laughs
On the wonderful plate where I still can see
The sea's enamel enclosed by the gold's pale copper!
Feather your oar on the forbidden waves!
The substance is closed: crack it open, Sesame!
And with your hands, always so noble and serene
On the treasures of the Kings plant the lilies of the Queens!
I would like to yoke my tastes to yours
Enshrine the beauty of Chartres and Amiens
Within meek copper or rebellious enamel.

L'œuvre sera plus difficile, mais plus belle
Le clocher revivra dans son ciel nuageux
Tu sauras retrouver les vitraux dans tes jeux
Mêle aux rubis de Reims les pierres de Venise.

The work will be more difficult, but more beautiful
The tower will stir again in its cloudy sky
You will rediscover the colored windows in your games
Mingle the stones of Venice with the rubies of Reims.

À Louisa de Mornand

Pour Louisa
(Le Ciel de Lit Couleur de Ciel,
L'Ange du Lit Couleur de Rose)

Couleur de ciel, le ciel du lit,
Azur strié de nuée blanche,
Flotte sur Louisa qui lit
Avant de dormir, sur la hanche.

Son attention certes faiblit :
Sa tête sommeilleuse penche,
Regardant sans voir une branche.
Que Madeleine Lemaire pinxit.

Sous prétexte que c'est dimanche
Marcel Proust, dans ce paradis
Duquel un ange se penche,
Est tant resté . . . que c'est lundi !

Du calice le plus pur de la manche
(Du tissu le plus fin ourdi)
D'un geste beau quoique engourdi
Le bras de Louisa, tige blanche
S'évase, monte, et resplendit.

Si j'ai dit qu'un ange se penche
De ce paradis si troublant,
Descendant du ciel bleu et blanc
Sur la vierge rose et blanche,

83

TO LOUISA DE MORNAND

FOR LOUISA
(THE BED CANOPY SKY-COLORED,
THE ANGEL OF THE BED ROSE-COLORED)

Sky-colored, the canopy of the bed,
An azure streaked with white cloud,
Floats over Louisa who reads
Lying on her side, before sleep.

Her attention falters:
Her somnolent head hangs,
Gazing blindly at a branch.
If only Madeleine Lemaire had painted it.

Under the pretext that it is Sunday
In this paradise from which
An angel hangs, Marcel Proust
Stayed so long that . . . it's Monday!

From the purest calyx of the sleeve
(Woven from the finest fabric)
With a gesture at once handsome and numb
The arm of Louisa, a white stem,
Flares, rises, and beams.

If I said an angel hangs
From this enticing paradise,
Descending from a sky of azure and white
Onto a virgin of blush and white

Je me suis sans doute mépris
Car c'est deux amours de Sèvres
Qui délicieux et surpris
Regardent s'unir des lèvres
Et deux cœurs qui se sont compris.

L'huis du salon entr'ouvert
Laisse voir la tenture rouge . . .
Le bleu de Tunis semble vert . . .
....

Le lit est bleu, le salon rouge
L'on n'entend plus rien qui bouge
Cher écrin de pourpre et d'azur
Tu renfermes une perle rose
....

I'm completely mistaken
Because it's two lovers of Sèvres
Delicious and surprised
Who watch lips come together
And two hearts interweave.

The half-open door of the salon
Offers a view of the red hangings . . .
The Tunisian blue seems green . . .
....

The bed is blue, the room red
One no longer hears anything move.
Dear jewel box of azure and purple
You contain a pink pearl
....

84

À Antoine Bibesco

C'est là : La Mer sans cesse
aux rochers de Porphyre

C'est la ; selon que souffle Eurus bise ou Zéphyre
Le flot par nous élu, aux rochers de porphyre
Brise son émeraude ou jette son saphir
Et laisse en s'enfuyante mille perles d'Ophir.

Près des vieux remparts roux, à l'ombre du menhir
Nous vivons de pain bis, de crème et de képhyr
Nous vivons comme Hugo, Tolstoï et Rousseau firent
Mais ton éternité ne pourrait nous suffire

Ô Dieu, si nous voulions devant les vagues bleues
Dérouler sur la toile ou redire à l'écho
Des rêves parcourus les innombrables lieues.

Car nos esprits puissants prompts comme la tempête
Visitent l'univers de sa base à son faîte
Nous nous nommons X et Antoine Bibesco.

84

TO ANTOINE BIBESCO

THERE! THE SEA UNCEASING AT THE ROCKS OF PORPHYRE

There! whether blows Eurus, the north, or Zephyr
Our chosen wave on rocks of Porphyre
Breaks its emerald or casts its sapphire
And releases a thousand pearls of Ophir.

By old reddish ramparts, in the shade of the menhir
We live on darkish bread, cream, and kefir
We live like Hugo, Tolstoy and Rousseau dear
But your eternity comes nowhere near.

Oh God, if we wanted before waves so blue
To unroll on the canvas or repeat in echo
The innumerable places of dreams gone through.

For our minds powerful and prompt as the storm
Visit the universe in its entire form
We call ourselves X and Antoine Bibesco.

85

ACROSTICHE

Baigne dans ton regard l'Univers fraternel
Immerge en ton Désir les êtres et les choses
Brandis les monts ainsi que l'on jette une rose
Et ton geste de Dieu, en blessant un mortel
Sous tes yeux enchantés nuancera de rose
Celui qui sous ton pied clama ton avenir.
Ô garde-lui du moins un tendre souvenir.

85

ACROSTIC

Bathe in your gaze the Universe fraternal
Immerse beings, things, as your Desire goes
Brandish the mountains as one throws a rose
E'en your Godly gesture wounding a mortal
So your enchanted eyes will tint rose
Certainly he who modestly saw your future as seer
Oh keep for him at least a sweet souvenir.

La « *Lutte* » avait été très chaude ; la victoire
Se prélassait au fond d'un ciel irradié
Quand, après un permis d'approcher *mendié*
Vers celui qui dormait dans l'or et dans la gloire

Nonelef miniscule, étroit, incendié
Par l'âpre jalousie où flamboyait sa poire
Veut le féliciter, sans joie on peut le croire,
Du drame à Marcel de Porto-Riche dédié.

Mais le héros vainqueur souriait sans colère
Au visage enfantin dont la prunelle est claire
La franchise apparente et le regard sournois.

Il rêvait à Colette ou riait à Suzanne
Remerciait *Parny* d'avoir sauvé sa *panne*
Et pressait les deux seins d'Hélène en tapinois.

The *"Fight"* had been quite hot; victory
Lounged under an irradiated sky
When, after permission to approach *begging*
Him who has slept in the gold and the glory

Miniscule Nonelef, narrow, steaming
From hard jealousy and with his fat face flaming—
Wants to congratulate him (joylessly, as we know),
For the drama Porto-Riche dedicated to Marcel.

But the conquering hero smiled without ire
At the baby face whose pupil is clear
The artful regard and apparent sincerity.

He dreamt of Colette or laughed at Suzanne
Thanked *Parny* for saving his *panne*
And squeezed Helen's two breasts on the sly.

Mon cœur plus qu'au rosier la tenace cétoine
Adhérait à l'espoir de voir venir Antoine
Je sentais l'horizon, j'interrogeais l'écho
Hélas la nuit passa sans que vînt Bibesco
Qui voulait me priver moi faible ismaélite
Parce que *Jacques Abram* n'a conquis que l'élite.
Encor ne faudrait-il pas dire Jacques *Abram*
Ose me reprocher cet auteur ridicule
Comme si quand un juif ou quand un chrétien prend
Un nom, que ce soit avec ou sans particule,
Il consulte d'abord la chanson de Roland,
L'histoire des vieux mots de sieur Picot (Émile)
Ou de Bréal, ou de Petit de Julleville,
Il préfère plutôt que ça rime à Sabran.

87

My heart closer to a rose than the tenacious cétoine
Clinging to the hope of seeing Antoine
I sensed the horizon, I interrogated the echo
Alas, the night passed without seeing Bibesco
Who wanted to deprive me weak Ismailite
Because *Jacques Abram* has only won the elite.
Again we must not say that Jacques *Abram*
Dares reproach me that ridiculous writer
Much like when a Jew or a Christian assumes
A name, either with or without a title,
He first consults the Song of Roland,
The history of ancient words by Mister Picot (Émile)
Or de Bréal, or de Petit de Julleville,
He prefers above all the rhyme of Sabran.

88

À Emmanuel Bibesco

Épître en Vers Burlesques Pour Remercier Emmanuel Bibesco d'Avoir Donné à Marcel Proust l'Adresse de Marthe Bibesco

Faire assavoir à la princesse
Qu'elle est belle et géniale (sic)
De cela je n'ai pas de cesse
Mais où écrire, c'est le hic ?

Nohant où fut Sand et Amic
Serait une adresse immortelle
Proche de nous et digne d'elle ;
Ou dans mon auto (marque Unic) . . .

Mais la France en Mars n'est pas chic,
Et plus loin elle a pris son clic,
Écrivons-lui donc qu'elle est belle :
Mais où l'écrire ? C'est le hic.

Balzac situait à Pornic
Entre les fleurs de basilic
L'illustre Aurore, poétesse

Et pour l'aimable Ferrari
Dont le censeur sévère a ri
Le moindre Stourdza est Altesse.

Altesse (louchez, Ô Soltyck)
Celle qu'à *Tristan* (par Van Dyck)
Mes yeux voulaient célibataire

88

To Emmanuel Bibesco

An Epistle in Burlesque Verse to Thank Emmanuel Bibesco for Having Given Marcel Proust Marthe Bibesco's Address

Writing to let the princess know
That she's lovely and brilliant (sic)
Is a task I can't let go,
But where to mail it, that's the trick?

Nohant where Sand dallied with Amic
Would be a simply divine address
Worthy of her and close to us;
Or in my motorcar (brand Unic) . . .

But France in March is hardly chic
And farther off she's lured her clique,
So let's write her that she's gorg-e-ous—
But where to write her? That's the trick.

Balzac imagined in Pornic
Among the basil flowers thick
Noble Aurora, the poetess

And Ferrari, sweetly daft,
At whom the grim-faced censor laughed
Calls every little Stourdza "Highness."

Your Highness (squint if you like, Soltyck),
She whom for *Tristan* (by Van Dyck)
My eyes preferred the single state

Et qu'Eustaziu ou Popesco
Nicolaïde ou Grescesco
Visiteront seuls, dans sa terre.

And whom Eustaziu or Popescu
Nicolaïde or Gresesco
Alone will visit in her estate.

À Bertrand de Fénelon

Eusses-tu la valeur dont s'illustre Enguerrand
La Toison de Colchos ou les arts de Médée
Ne crois pas que par toi soit jamais possédée
La rare amitié du Vicomte Bertrand.

Son charme, dit Antoine, est délicat et grand
Blum est du même avis et c'est aussi l'idée
Du rongeur taciturne à l'âme si bridée
Que l'esprit paternel à sa bouche surprend.

Nul eut-il nom Lorris, Jouvenel, Hahn ou Vite
Casqué d'or héraldique ou ceint de la lévite
Ne charme son esprit inutilement beau.

Mais prodige charmant où l'être se révèle
En chaque esprit ardent, le sien comme un flambeau
Allume et fait briller une flamme nouvelle.

89

To Bertrand de Fénelon

Even with the daring of Enguerrand,
The Golden Fleece, or Queen Medea's skill,
Don't imagine you possess or ever will
The precious friendship of Vicomte Bertrand.

Grand and refined, says Antoine, are his charms;
Blum thinks the same, and that's also supposed
By the taciturn bookworm with a soul so composed
That the fatherly spirit in his lips so warms.

No one, even with the name Lorris, Juvenal, Hahn or Vite,
Helmeted in heraldic gold or in a riding coat from Rogers Peet
Enchants his uselessly beautiful mind.

But charming prodigy whose being gleams
In ardent wit, his like a torch of some kind
Illumines and kindles ever new flames.

Fais fermenter ce soir la vigne ou le houblon
La Bière de Bohême ou le vin de Champagne
Car l'ami délicat, que la Muse accompagne,
Vient déjeuner demain, Bertrand de Fénelon.

90

At night ferment the grapes or hops
Fix Bohemian beer or elixir of Champagne,
My fine friend, companion of the Muse
Comes for lunch tomorrow—Bertrand de Fénelon.

Que le repas soit bref ; poulet froid et melon
Quelques roses de France un peu de vin d'Espagne
Et des fruits apportés tout frais de la campagne
Humides de rosée ou piqués de frelons

Après loin de Tracy, d'Hahn ou d'Albufera
Augurant de cela qui fut, ce qui sera
Écoute sa pensée alerte et prophétique

Et vois ce Fénelon à qui Mentor sourit
Pour sa verve subtile et son précoce esprit,
Ajouter un rameau vivace à l'arbre antique.

91

Let the meal be simple: cold chicken, melon sorbets
A few French roses a drop of Spanish wine
And ripe country fruits picked just in time
Wet with dew or stung by hornets

After, far from Tracy-sur-Mer, Albufera or Hahn
Foreshadowing that which was, and what will dawn
Listen to his keen thoughts and prophecies

And watch this Fénelon, on whom Mentor smiles
For all his subtle verve and precocious wiles,
Add a living branch to the ancient tree.

En Passant Avenue Malakoff

Lisant les hauts faits de Thérèse ou d'Aurignac
Dans *Le Temps*, son austère et géante gazette,
Beau, l'œil dardé tel qu'on peint le divin musagète
Vois, près de son bureau Bertrand de Salignac.

Contre le Turc, le Juif, le Maure ou l'Armagnac
Jadis Preux et faisant voler fronde ou sagette
Il aurait ignoré le Pinde et le Taygète,
Mais il va lire Ovide en buvante un cognac.

Comment lui plairais-tu ? Tu n'es ni beau, ni riche
De cet esprit subtil, charmeur et filial
Dont est fier à bon droit Marcel de Porto-Riche.

Tente pourtant l'accès de ce cœur lilial
Nulle amitié ne passe en douceur la sienne
Où survit comme une grace fénelonienne.

92

PASSING BY AVENUE MALAKOFF

Reading the heroic deeds of Thérèse or Aurignac
In *Le Temps*, his huge, sober chronicle of news,
Handsome, his eyes like Apollo leading the Muse,
Behold, near his desk, Bertrand de Salignac.

Against Turk, Jew, Moor or Armagnac
Flinging catapults or arrows like a hero of yore,
He would have scaled Pindus or Taygetus as a trifling chore,
But in our day he reads Ovid and sips his cognac.

How could you satisfy him? You're neither handsome nor rich
With that filial, charming, and subtle wit
That is the pride of Marcel de Porto-Riche.

So, you should try to win your way into that lily-like heart
Because no friendship is sweeter than his
In which a grace like Fénelon's still plays its part.

À Louis d'Albufera

Marcel s'est demandé : qu'est-ce qu'Albu fera ?
Il me semble ce soir désirer qu'on roupille.
Pourtant Louisa, mon cher, est vraiment belle fille,
Et n'adore ici-bas que Louis d'Albufera.

Louisa l'a regardé de son œil qui pétille
Et dit, en se leurrant : ce soir Louis m'aimera.
—Peut-être, simplement, Albu roupillera
Et le marqueur de coups ne verra pas la bille
Docile au coup de queue énergique et tremblant
Commencer en branlant sa folle sarabande
Et frémissant de jolie accourir vers la bande
Avant que le queuteur l'ait touché de son blanc.

Louisa nous semble à tous une pure déesse
Son corps n'en doutez pas doit tenir la promesse
De ses deux yeux rêveurs, malicieux et doux ;
Mais de la posséder nous n'aurons pas l'ivresse
Si même nous voulions l'en prier à genoux ;
Nous pourrons la revoir et la chérir sans cesse
Mais ce trésor hélas, ne sera pas à nous.

De ce corps merveilleux je n'ai vu que la tête,
D'un maître impérieux il reste la conquête
Et seul il peut régner sur ce festin si beau
Et peut-être tous deux vous plaindrez ma tristesse,
Et penserez que j'ai dans l'âme une détresse

To Louis d'Albufera

Marcel asked himself: what will Albufera do?
Tonight I feel that one longs to slumber.
Yet—my dear friend—Louisa's a hot number,
And loves no one on this earth like she loves you.

Louisa glanced his way with a sparkling eye
And said, deluding herself: tonight Louis will love me.
—But perhaps Albu will just catch some Zs—
And the billiard ball will pass the scorekeeper by
Submissive at the shaky but forceful cue's shot
It starts with a wobble those crazy dance moves
And quivering with joy rolls toward the cushions
Before the cue-wielder has made his bank shot.

Of course we all think Louisa's a pure goddess
Her body (don't doubt it) must answer the promise
Of her two dreaming eyes, malicious and tender;
But we're not so drunk as to think we can possess
Her, even had we wanted to pray to her powers;
We can cherish the vision of her forever
But this treasure, alas, shall never be ours.

I've only seen the head of her marvelous physique—
It awaits to be conquered by an imperial master
He alone will reign over this superfine feast
Then maybe both of you will pity my sadness
And believe that my soul remains in distress,

A rester malheureux jusqu'au jour du tombeau,
(Non pas de ces « tombeaux » qu'on entrouve
   sans cesse
Pour en faire sortir les secrets enfouis,
Mais de celui qui tous à la suprême messe
Bertrand, Jeanne, Louisa, Marcel, Antoine, Louis
Combien d'autres amis, inconnus, ennemis,
A tout jamais nous gardera, ensevelis.)

Amis, vous vous trompez, c'est sans mélancolie
Que je vois vos amours passer si près de moi
Et la fierté d'Albu, le seul enviable roi
Le seul fou dont chacun approuve la folie.

Amis, c'est sans regrets, amis, c'est sans douleur
Que je vois comme un papillon sur une fleur
Vos baisers éperdus se poser sur sa bouche,

Albu c'est sans douleur que je pense à la couche
Où (tandis qu'un nez mince, ironique et lassé
Se plaint que le sirop n'était pas très glacé
Chez Larue, de qui les harengs ne sont pas bates,
Ou le sublime Henry dont vous me régalâtes)
Vous étreignez le corps longuement caressé
Parfois même portant la purpurine touche
D'un ongle un peu brutal ou d'un poing trop farouche !

Albu, c'est sans regrets, car un jour ancien
Je compris que votre bonheur était le sien
Et j'ai fait consister le mien à voir le vôtre
Ne pouvant demander à Louisa rien d'autre
Que de vous rendre heureux Louis uniquement
Vous son ami fidèle et son unique amant.

Consigned to unhappiness until in the tomb
(Not the "tomb" of silence we open nonstop
To let our buried secrets out—
But the tomb that will watch over all of us—
Bertrand, Jeanne, Louisa, Marcel, Antoine, Louis,
And who knows how many other friends, unknown,
  hostile—
at that final mass forever and ever, six feet under).

Friend, you are mistaken, I feel no melancholy
Watching your love affairs pass me so closely by
And Albufera's pride, the only king we envy—
The only fool for whom we all approve the folly.

Friend, dear friend, it is neither with regret nor pain
That I see, like a butterfly landing on a flower
Your desperate kisses placed upon her mouth,

Albu it is without pain that I think of the bed
Where (while a thin nose, weary and wry,
whines that the syrup wasn't adequately iced
Chez Larue, where the herrings are not packed,
or Henry—the sublime place you took me)
You embrace that body with a lingering caress
Sometimes even touching the purplish crimson
With nail a tad brutal or a too aggressive fist!

Albu, I have no regrets, for one day long ago
I understood that your happiness was my own
And that my own is secured by securing yours
I can ask of Louisa nothing more than to make you,
and you alone, a happy man, Louis Albufera
you her faithful friend and you her only lover.

Mon amitié pour vous, délicate et fidèle
Eût tué pour toujours le moindre amour pour elle
Si jamais il avait dû naître dans mon cœur
Où vous avez, mon cher, ce que j'ai de meilleur.

My friendship for you, so delicate and true
Has killed for all time any feeling I had for her
If ever it had been born in my heart
Where you possess, my dear friend, the best part.

94

AU COMTE GREFFULHE

Hélas il partira demain pour Boisboudran
Où le soleil mourant charme l'eau qui le pleure
D'un baiser sans chaleur et d'un rayon d'une heure
Et son génie hâtif y grandira d'un cran.

Sans cesse il croît : il est l'inoubliable écran
Où les matins joyeux, où les soirs où l'on pleure
Viennent poser leur flamme ou dévoiler leur leurre
Et dit exactement les jours comme un cadran.

Aussi l'or pâlissant de ce limpide automne
Teindra d'un jade exquis cette âme qui m'étonne
Nous verrons refleurir en vers ce jour défunt

Et peut-être le soir au versant des paroles
J'en sentirai renaître et monter le parfum
Comme d'un encensoir ou d'une parabole.

94

FOR COUNT GREFFULHE

Tomorrow, alas, to Bois-Boudran he's away,
Where the dying sun charms the water that weeps
With a tepid kiss and an hour's worth of ray,
While his swift genius grows in measured leaps.

Ceaselessly it grows: it is the constant screen
Where the joyful morns and evenings when one weeps
Come rest their flame or manifest their schemes
And, like a sundial, mark off time's grand sweep.

Thus the pale gold of this limpid season
Will tint in lovely jade this wondrous mind.
In verse we'll see this dying day re-risen

And at night, perhaps, on speech's underside
I'll feel its perfume reemerge and climb
As from a censer or parabola.

95

À LA COMTESSE GREFFULHE

Hélas Élisabeth de Caraman-Chimay
Qu'Arman de Caillavet, têtu comme une mule
S'obstine à dénommer Comtesse *de* Greffulhe.

....

Vous avez bien raison de recevoir en Mai
Puisque vous posséder un fort riche pécule
D'ailleurs votre esprit peine et volontiers spécule
Et vos yeux inondés sont de ceux que j'aimai

Mais dans ce triste jour dédoré de Novembre
Qui meurt dans le chagrin, dans la fourrure et l'ambre
N'aurait-il pas suffi de Turenne ou d'Hermant

Et pourquoi voulez-vous, marchant sur mes brisées
Arracher à mon cœur que charment vos pensées
Pour un jour tout entier l'auteur du *Bon Amant*.

95

To Comtesse Greffulhe

Alas Élisabeth de Caraman-Chimay
Whom Arman de Caillavet, stubborn as a mule
Persists in calling Comtesse *de* Greffulhe.

....

In May time you're right to hold your at-homes
Since you have so much wealth in store
And your mind strains to invest yet more
And your brimming eyes are those I loved once.

But on this bleak November day, all gold leaves gone,
Now dying in despond, in amber and fur muff
Wouldn't Turenne or Hermant have been enough?

You've poached on my grounds—why do you want
To tear from my heart (charmed by your thoughts
For an entire day) the author of *Le Bon Amant*?

À Jean Cocteau

Dans ton Midi pour ces raisons je t'écris, Jean :
Le silence est de plomb, la parole d'argent
Et les mots font du bien où l'on voit l'effigie
De l'Amitié ou de Minerve ou bien . . . d'Hygie.
Donc reçois tous ceux-ci comme maigre salaire
De ton charme vivant qui sait si bien me plaire.
D'abord prose : tu sais homme talentueux
M'imaginant Verlainien et fastueux
Tu m'as écrit sur du papier du Mercure
Pour joindre aux boulingrins un faune dont n'a cure
Ton ami qui n'est pas si féru de Verlaine
Et grogne s'il lui faut ouvrir son bas de laine
Aussi je n'envoyai, Jean, que cinquante francs.
Mais j'ai honte. Faut-il doubler, tripler ? Sois franc.
Autre chose, j'irai voir *Maman Colibri*.
Parmi les jeunes gens flos libri :
Quels sont intéressants (j'entends intéressés)
En dehors du classique et charmant Puylagarde
Un peu Forain pour moi dans sa face hagarde.
Peut-on sentir de près les roses et les lys
De celui dont le nom hélas est Cazalis
Et recevoir cela de Monteaux, de Jean Kern
Que j'appelais enfant du fromage à la Kern.

96

TO JEAN COCTEAU

This is why I'm writing you at your southern place, Jean:
Silence is lead, speech silver
And words do such good where one sees the effigy
Of friendship or of Minerva or even of Hygeia.
So receive these as humble wages
Of your living charm, which knows so well how to
    please me.
First of all, prose: you know, talented man,
Imagining that I'm Verlainian and sumptuous,
You wrote me on a page of the *Mercure*
To add to bowling greens a faun about which your friend,
Who isn't so keen on Verlaine, could care less.
And he grumbles if he has to open his nest egg.
So I sent only fifty francs, Jean,
And am ashamed. Should I double or triple it? Be frank.
Another thing: I'm going to see *Maman Colibri*.
Among young people flos libri:
Which are interesting (I mean interested)
Apart from classic and charming Puylagarde
Whose haggard face is like a Forain's.
Can you smell up close the roses and lilies
From him whose name, alas, is Cazalis
And receive them from Jean Kern in Monteaux,
Whom I called a child of Cheese à la Kern.

Afin de me couvrir de fourrure et de moire
Sans de ses larges yeux renverser l'encre noire
Tel un sylphe au plafond, tel sur la neige un ski
Jean sauta sur la table auprès de Nijinsky.
C'était dans un salon purpurin de Larue
Dont l'or, d'un goût douteux, jamais ne se voila.
La barbe d'un docteur blanditieuse et drue
Déclarait : « Ma présence est peut-être incongrue
Mais s'il n'en reste qu'un je serai celui-là. »
Et mon cœur succombait aux coups d'*Indiana*.

97

And so to cover myself with fur and silk,
Without his large eyes spilling black ink
Like a sylph on the ceiling or a ski on snow,
Jean jumped on the table next to Nijinsky.
It was in a purplish room of Larue
In which gold, in dubious taste, always glared.
The doctor's thick and caressing beard
Said: "My presence is perhaps incongruous
But if only one is left I'll be that one."
And my heart succumbed to the strains of *Indiana*.

98

À Armand de Gramont

Au Duc de Guiche
Impromptu Généalogique
pour Mirliton

Au cher Vicomte de Larboust
Beaucoup de gré sait Marcel Proust
Car sans ce bon Garcia Sanche
Je ne pourrais pas ce dimanche
Écrire le nom d'Armand d'Aure
Et lui répéter que j'adore
L'esprit exquis dont n'est pas chiche
Ce dixième (?) Duc de Guiche

To Armand de Gramont

To the Duc de Guiche
A Genealogical Impromptu
For Mirliton

To the dear Vicomte de Larboust
Many thanks are due from Marcel Proust
For without Garcia Sanche the gay
I could not on this Sabbath day
Write the name of Armand d'Aure
And repeat to him that I adore
The exquisite wit which is so rich
In the tenth (I reckon) Duc de Guiche

99

Ici Demeure Armand de Gramont

Duc de Guiche

* *

Changeant cent fois d'aspect comme fait « Little Tiche »
Nous apparaît Armand de Gramont, duc de Guiche
Il ne lui suffit pas d'être escrimeur et duc

Et peintre, pour qui vous restez roses, Ô roses !
Il se penche souvent sur l'abîme des causes.
Sans doute quand flûté par le soir musical
Un rose harmonieux sur le château ducal

Chante sa mélodie au ciel qu'il ensanglante
Guiche d'un fin coup d'œil note sa chanson lente
Hautbois délicieux ou mystique (. . .)
Qu'un jour il transcrira aux marges d'un pastel

* *

Sous le peintre s'insurge un chimiste indocile
L'un étudie un ton, l'autre la chlorophylle

* *

Passant, que ce décor majestueux aguiche
Regarde avec respect ce formidable hôtel
Ici demeure Armand de Gramont, duc de Guiche

Here Dwells Armand de Gramont
Duc de Guiche

* *

Changing his looks a hundred times like "Little Tiche"
He appears to us as Armand de Gramont, Duc de Guiche.
It is not enough for him to be swordsman and duke

And painter, for whom ye flourish pink, ye roses!
He often peers into the abyss of causes,
His *soirée musicale* casts quite a glow
Of harmonious rose-pink over the ducal château,

Sings its melody to the sky it turns bloodred.
Guiche with expert glance notes the song's slow tread—
Oboe, delicious or mystical! . . .
One day he will transfer it to the edge of a pastel.

* *

Behind the painter rears up a stubborn chemist
One studies chiaroscuro, the other, chlorophyll

* *

Passersby, enticed by this majestic frame,
Gaze respectfully on this magnificent pile
Here dwells Duc Armand de Gramont, the same.

L'art d'à jamais fixer un contour immortel
Il l'apprit de Lévy, Durand et de Leriche
Et d'Ayat l'art charmant de lancer un cartel

Mais au double pinceau traversé d'une épée
Dont s'écartèle ici le cimier ducal
Vois, imprévu rameau du tronc patriarcal
La pointe d'un compas finement découpée

* *

Mais silence un bonheur plus pur est sur ses jours
Et sûr de sa livrée immortelle et jolie
On dit que lui sourit divinement Thalie
Sous les traits de Vénus et qu'enchaîne l'Amour

Ici demeure Armand de Gramont, duc de Guiche

The art of establishing forever an immortal style—
From Lévy, Durand and Leriche he learned that game
And from Ayat the charming art of sneering with a smile.

Brush and sabre crossed in saltire
Ornament the ducal crest, but see
An unforeseen branch of the family tree:
The pointed compass maths require.

　　　　* *

But silence! A purer happiness rests on his days,
He's sure of his immortal plumage and his song,
They say Muse Thalia smiles divinely on his ways
In the guise of Venus stringing Love along

Here dwells Armand de Gramont, Duc de Guiche

À Celeste

Grande, fine, belle, un peu maigre,
Tantôt lasse, tantôt allègre,
Charmant les princes et la pègre,
Lançant à Marcel un mot aigre,
Rendant pour le miel le vinaigre,
Spirituelle, agile, intègre
C'est la presque nièce de Nègre.

For Celeste

Tall and slender, fair and thin,
Sometimes up, sometimes all in,
Charming princes and bedouin,
With Marcel she's hard as sin,
Repays his honey with aspirin,
Witty, agile, sharp as a pin:
Such is Albert Nègre's kin.

Sombres chagrins des ciels coutumièrement gris
Plus tristes d'être bleus aux rares éclaircies
Et qui laissant alors sur les plaines transies
Filtrer les tièdes pleurs d'un soleil incompris
Auxillac, Ô morose humeur des plaines sombres
Qui s'étendent sans fin, sans joie et sans couleurs,
La Canourgue au lointain répand ses larges ombres,
Les maigres jardinets ne portent pas de fleurs.
François-Régis, tirant ses seaux, rentre et chétive,
Sa jument résignée, anxieuse et rêvant,
En dressant par instants sa cervelle pensive
Hume d'un souffle lourd le souffle fort du vent.

Somber sorrows of skies usually gray
Sadder to be the rare blue of clearings
That leaving on transient chilled plains
Filter the lukewarm tears of a misunderstood sun.
Auxillac, O gloomy mood of dark plains
That stretch endlessly, colorless and without joy,
Canourgue spreads its broad shadows in the distance,
The meager gardens have no flowers.
Sickly François-Régis returns, carrying his buckets, and his
   scrawny,
Resigned mare, anxious and dreaming,
Raising at intervals its pensive head
With a deep breath inhales a gust of wind.

102

À Paul Morand

Ode à Paul Morand

Cher ami, quelle est cette Lampe à Arc
Qui vous a empêché d'aller aux Fêtes de Jeanne d'Arc . . .
N'est-ce pas inconcevable je l'ai trouvé avec du feu
Du reste il (Proust) devient de jour en jour plus gâteux.

(Extrait de mon Ode à Paul Morand
laquelle ne sera pas publiée)

102

To Paul Morand

Ode to Paul Morand

Dear friend, what is this Lampe à Arc
That has kept you from going to the Fêtes de Jeanne d'Arc
Isn't it incredible that I found it with fire
Besides, he (Proust) spoils more each day and soon will
 expire.

(Excerpt from my Ode to Paul Morand
 which will not be published)

« Ah ! Que son port est beau et que noble son geste
Deux "ne m'oubliez pas" lui servent de regard
Si vous devez partir, jusqu'à votre départ
Qu'elle reste
Céleste
Archange hebdomadaire où l'on voit la couleur
Rose d'une fleur ».

103

Ah! How lovely her bearing, how noble her zest,
Two forget-me-nots form her regard.
Until your departure, if indeed you must part,
Let her rest,
Céleste
Weekly archangel in whom one sees the color
Pink of a flower.

À Jean Boissonnas

En tes cheveux revit l'automne :
Son charme triste et somptueux
Luit dans l'éclat monotone
Mélancolique et somptueux
      De tes cheveux

Mais le printemps mystérieux
Vert et lumineux qui nous donne
Les reflets les plus précieux
Dont notre œil jouit et s'étonne
Ravit aussi dans ta personne
      C'est le pâle or vert de tes yeux.

104

To Jean Boissonnas

In your hair autumn itself revives,
Its charm, sad and sumptuous,
Shines out amid monotoned lives,
So melancholy and sumptuous,
     from your hair.

But spring so mysterious
Green and luminous that gives us
Reflections so precious,
Which thrills us, surprising our eyes,
Delighting, too, in your face,
     The pale gold green of your eyes.

Proust's drawing that
accompanied Poem 36,
sent to Reynaldo Hahn
from Dordrecht.

Proust's drawing that
accompanied Poem 37,
sent to Reynaldo Hahn
from Dordrecht.

Proust's drawing that
accompanied Poem 58.

Notes

Marcel Proust read footnotes.

—Robert Dreyfus

These notes are meant to give the reader the information that the poem's reader (or, when the poem was sent to an individual, the recipient) would have had at the time or a bit of relevant archival information. Because many of them were scrawled on envelopes, on the back of letters from other people, and even in books, they often included "variantes," possible differences that resulted from Proust experimenting with the verses and neglecting to erase his abortions. For readers who would like to see the variantes and other brief textual information, read *Poèmes*, compiled by Francis and Gontier.

In the notes, to avoid long repetition, I have followed tradition and abbreviated *À la recherche du temps perdu* (*Remembrance of Things Past* or *In Search of Lost Time*) as RTP. Please note that real people have often been described as "models" for characters in RTP, but almost all of RTP's characters are composites. Proust appropriated various traits of people of the time, later filtering them through his aesthetic lens. Publication information for books referenced in the notes can be found in the "Suggestions for Further Reading" section. References to "Kolb" mean Proust's *Correspondance*, edited by Philip Kolb. References to "Tadié" mean *Proust: A Biography* by Jean-Yves Tadié.

We also decided not to include line numbers, which would make the poems seem like museum pieces. The poems should be short enough for readers to easily find the line references made in these notes.

Poems 1, 2, 4, and 6 were discovered in the Daniel Halévy archive in Dijon and published in *Marcel Proust: Écrits de jeunesse 1887–1895*, edited by Anne Borrel et al. Poems 3 and 5 and 7 through 102 were published in the *Cahiers Marcel Proust: Poèmes*, edited by Francis and Gontier. Poems 103 and 104 are reprinted from unpublished autograph letters. Please note that wherever possible I have corrected Proust's misspellings of proper names.

POEM 1

Translated by Richard Howard

Most likely composed in November 1888 and dedicated to Daniel Halévy (see notes to Poem 3). It seems to have elicited a correction from Halévy, since Proust responded with a letter discussing Halévy's correction, which was truncated when Proust's philosophy teacher, Alphonse Darlu, interrupted its writing. See Marcel Proust, *Écrits de jeunesse*, pp. 150–51.

Proust's sexuality was a matter of public discussion even during his lifetime, but this poem and letters between Proust and Jacques Bizet and Daniel Halévy written at the same time certainly make his interest in homosexuality abundantly clear. In a letter to Bizet, probably written in the spring of 1888, he responds to Bizet's letter (now lost) that seems to say that Bizet had refused Proust's advances, Proust saying that he is "not fatuous enough to believe that my body is so precious a treasure that to renounce it required great strength of character . . . Still, I always find it sad not to pluck the delicious flower that we shall soon be unable to pluck. For then it would be fruit . . . and forbidden." Proust writes to Halévy later in the year, "You think me jaded and effete. You are mistaken. If you are delicious, if you have lovely eyes which reflect the grace and refinement of your mind with such purity that I feel I cannot fully love your mind without kissing your eyes, if your body and mind, like your thoughts, are so lithe and slender that I feel I could mingle more intimately with your thoughts by sitting on your lap, if, finally, I feel that the charm of your person, in which I cannot separate your keen mind from your agile body, would refine and enhance 'the sweet joy of love' for me, there is nothing in all that to deserve your contemptuous words, which would have been more fittingly addressed to someone surfeited with women and seeking new pleasures in pederasty." (Letter translated by Terrence Kilmartin.) At about that time, Halévy wrote in his journal, "Take Proust. As talented as they come and yet look at how he overdoes it. Weak, young, he screws, he masturbates, maybe he even pederasts! But maybe in his life he'll show flashes of hidden genius."

POEM 2

Translated by Cole Swensen

Found in Daniel Halévy's hand in his journal and dated May 10, 1889, preceded by the word "Proust: Vers à Laure Hayman." For more information, see *Écrits de jeunesse 1887–1895*, pp. 153–54.

According to the *Bénézit Dictionary of Artists*, Laure Hayman (1851–1932) was born in Valparaiso, Chile; according to Georges Andrieux's introduction in *Lettres et vers à Mesdames Laure Hayman et Louisa de Mornand*, she was born in the Cordillera of the Andes, in the Hacienda La Mariposa. Her grandfather was the painter Francis Hayman, who had taught Thomas Gainsborough. Her father was an engineer who died at a young age, after which her mother gave piano lessons to support them.

Hayman has been variously described as a "cocotte," a word that literally means "little hen" (it's also a type of casserole) but was widely used for a "kept woman," a "demi-mondaine," and a "courtesan," the type of personage depicted in Émile Zola's

Nana (1880). Cocottes were well-known social and cultural fig-
ures of the time (among them one might include Méry Laurent,
Liane de Pougy, and La Belle Otero), who demanded a modicum
of independence from their patrons in return for sexual and so-
cial liaisons. A portrait of Hayman by Philadelphia-born painter
Julius LeBlanc Stewart (1855–1919), completed in 1882 when the
subject was thirty-one years old, depicts her seated, slim and
beautiful in a colorful, frilly dress, a dainty foot set atop a pil-
low, but photographs by Nadar taken only two years earlier
show her as more robust and sober.

Twenty years his senior, when Proust met her in the 1880s
Hayman was the mistress of his great-uncle Louis Weil (his
mother's uncle in whose Auteuil house Proust was born). Their
initial meeting—real or imagined—probably led to the scene in
Swann's Way in which the narrator comes upon The Lady in
Pink at his great-uncle Adolphe's apartment. She may also have
been Proust's father's mistress for a brief time, though this has
never been proven. When Weil died, for reasons of propriety
Laure was unable to attend the funeral, but she sent a wreath,
which Proust's mother herself placed on top of her uncle's coffin,
though in the Jewish tradition the rituals of death do not include
such objects. Well after Uncle Louis's death, Proust sent Hay-
man a vase of flowers and one of Louis's pins, as a keepsake.
Sending those flowers was not a new practice for Proust: in a
letter to Geneviève Straus in the early 1890s, Proust noted that
he had no money left for presents for her because all his money
was taken up with sending flowers to Mademoiselle Hayman.

Hayman was the model for the title character of the short
novel *Gladys Harvey* (1888) by Paul Bourget (1852–1935). Bour-
get even notes that the fictional Harvey had a "creole child-
hood." When Hayman and Proust became friends, she was so
taken with him that she made a cover for a gift copy of the novel
from a piece of her silk petticoats and sent it to him with the
inscription, "Ne rencontrez jamais une Gladys Harvey" (Stay
away from women like Gladys Harvey). Robert Dreyfus paints
a wonderful portrait of her and her relationship with the young
Proust, without mentioning her name (*Souvenirs*, pp. 43–46). In

her biography of Jeanne Proust, Evelyne Bloch-Dano quotes the painter Jacques-Emile Blanche, saying that "he was only seventeen, she was plump, but she had a slim waist and wore very low-cut dresses, decorated with dangling pearls (three rows on each side) barely covering her bosom. Her hair was ash-blond, braided with a pink ribbon; her eyes were black, and when she was very excited, they tended to open extremely wide" (translation by Alice Kaplan).

Hayman is also often believed to be a model for Odette in RTP, a notion given greater credence by the fact that she lived in rue La Pérouse, just off the Étoile in Paris, where Odette "was living" when she met Charles Swann. The comparison of the real Hayman and the fictional Odette only reaches so far, since apart from a few personal idiosyncrasies, Odette's lack of personal generosity never seemed to mirror the warmth that existed between Hayman and Proust, which Proust noted to friends when Hayman complained about Odette's portrayal in *Le Côté des Guermantes.*

In her forties, long past her prime as a cocotte, Hayman took up sculpture and soon thereafter began to exhibit small pieces in the Paris Salon, initiating a second career as a visual artist. Her work included a small, charming bronze of a dancing Isadora Duncan, which is currently in the permanent collection of the Legion of Honor Museum in San Francisco.

POEM 3

Translated by Susan Stewart

Though this sonnet was found in Daniel Halévy's hand in his journal, just after "Lines to Laure Hayman" (Poem 2), Halévy published it in his memoir *Pays Parisiens*—without noting that it was addressed to him—saying it had been written by Proust and adding, "Among the old papers I'm going through as I write, I found this sonnet addressed to one of us, and as I read it I experience something other than the bemusement of a childish memory: it's exquisite."

The Halévy family constituted cultural aristocracy in mid- and late-nineteenth century Paris and played a major role both in Proust's life and art. Daniel Halévy's great-grandfather Elie, the son of a rabbi and talented in music composition and choral conducting as well as literary exegesis, emigrated from Würzburg to Paris in the late eighteenth century. Elie had two sons, Fromental and Léon, both of whom achieved fame in Parisian artistic circles. The former would compose several highly acclaimed operas, including *La Juive*, which Proust would use as a prominent and recurring motif in *À la recherche du temps perdu*, beginning with the narrator's own grandfather humming an aria from the work when a friend of his grandson came to call, to the epithet the narrator gives to Rachel, the prostitute he frequents, "Rachel, quand du seigneur," who turns out later to be his best friend's great love.

Fromental's daughter, Geneviève, would play an important role in Proust's entry into Parisian artistic and social circles. At the age of twenty, Geneviève married the composer Georges Bizet, who was thirty at the time of the marriage. However, with the perceived failure of his 1875 opera *Carmen*, Bizet experienced a deep depression and then died of a heart attack, at the age of thirty-six. Proust, Bizet's son Jacques, and Daniel Halévy would all attend the Lycée Condorcet. For information on Jacques Bizet, see the notes to Poem 26. At Mme Straus's salon Proust would meet Paris's nobility, artists, writers, musicians, and wealthy businessmen, many of whom would later populate his work.

Proust and Daniel Halévy would remain close friends for many years, although they fell out with one another several times and had grown apart by the time they had reached their thirties. In his memoir *Souvenirs sur Marcel Proust* (Memories of Marcel Proust, 1926), Robert Dreyfus, Proust and Halévy's schoolmate at the Lycée Condorcet, described the uneasiness of their schoolboy relationship: "The difference in their natures: Marcel Proust's 'warmth and good will' tended to startle a colder, more closed, and defensive Daniel Halévy who then, following a show of mood and impatience, would, without even a backward glance, draw close to him again." In fact, Dreyfus mentions that at one point during their school days Halévy refused to speak to Proust for a month. Though Proust often claimed to have brought the novelist Anatole France into the (Alfred) Dreyfusard fold (see notes to Poem 74), Halévy should most likely share the credit, since the approach took place at a party at the Halévy home, and the following day France signed a petition on Dreyfus's behalf in the presence of them both.

Halévy went on to a respected career as an historian and editor.

POEM 4

Translated by Jeff Clark

See the note to Poem 3 for information on Daniel Halévy.

POEM 5

Translated by Cole Swensen

POEM 6

Translated by Deborah Treisman

Published in *Le Mensuel*, 1ère année, no. 5, fevrier 1891, pages 5–6, which also carried Proust's review of a series of lectures on the chanteuse Yvette Guilbert by Hugues Le Roux (pen name of journalist Robert C. Henri, who in 1889 had the distinction of being the first journalist to the top of the Eiffel Tower and later collaborated on a play with Proust's close friend Gaston Arman de Caillavet; see notes to Poem 8). For more information, see *Écrits de jeunesse 1887–1895*, edited by Anne Borrel.

The poem was dedicated to Proust's friend at the École Libre des sciences politiques Gustave Laurens de Waru (1871–1941), son of Comte Pierre Laurens de Waru and nephew of Comtesse Adhéaume de Chevigné, née Laure de Sade, a descendant of the notorious Marquis. At that time, Proust was trying his best to attract Madame de Chevigné's attention, going so far as to follow her walking-route in the street and then pretending to come upon her accidentally. An unflattering account of Proust's obsession appears in Princesse Marthe Bibesco's *Proust's Oriane*. Comtesse de Chevigné became one of Proust's models for the Duchesse de Guermantes in RTP, whose nephew was Robert de Saint-Loup, the narrator's best friend. Madame de Chevigné's son-in-law, Francis de Croisset (1877-1937), who had changed his name from Franz Wiener (choosing it for its associations with Flaubert and most likely to appear a bit more noble to his new aristocratic relations) wrote the libretto for Reynaldo Hahn's opera *Ciboulette* (1923) and was a good friend of Proust's.

In 1983, a portrait of the Comtesse by Federico de Madrazo y de Ochoa (1875–1934), a friend of Proust known as Coco, was donated to the Metropolitan Museum of Art by its then director, Philippe de Montebello. De Montebello is Comtesse Adhéaume de Chevigné's great-grandson.

Epigraph: Proust borrowed the phrase "Amants, amants heureux" (lovers, happy lovers) from a fable by Jean de La Fontaine (1621–1695), *Les Deux Pigeons* (*The Two Doves*), Book IX, fable 2, line 65. He also quoted it in a letter to Georges de Lauris written in October 1906.

Amants, heureux amants, voulez-vous voyager?
Que ce soit aux rives prochaines;
Soyez-vous l'un à l'autre un monde toujours beau,
Toujours divers, toujours nouveau;
Tenez-vous lieu de tout, comptez pour rien le reste.

Lovers, if happy, never idly roam;
Let all your travels be around your home.
Be to each other still a world, a prize;

Be new and various in each other's eyes,
And hence let daily scenes of bliss arise.

TRANSLATION OF LES DEUX PIGEONS
BY ROBERT THOMSON

POEM 7

Translated by Wayne Koestenbaum

Written on the back of a piece of paper on which Proust also wrote notes for classes in law, so it was probably composed around 1891, when Proust had recently matriculated as a law student.

POEM 8

Translated by Harold Augenbraum

Dedicated to Jeanne Pouquet, who played Cleopatra in a revue written by her future husband, Gaston Arman de Caillavet (1869–1915), probably in late 1890 or early 1891. Proust was the prompter for that evening. In his *Lives*, Plutarch notes that Cleopatra and Mark Antony met at Cydmus "in the time of life when women's beauty is most splendid, and their intellects are in full maturity."

As he often did with attached women, perhaps because there was little chance of an actual attachment for himself, Proust paid court to Pouquet, which enraged Caillavet, but the two were later reconciled. Jeanne appears in one of the better known photographs of Proust, in which Proust, on one knee, at an outing pretends to "strum" a tennis racquet and serenade the young Pouquet, who is standing on a chair. According to André Maurois, delicate health prevented Proust from playing sports, so "the refreshments were his department." While Proust served his obligatory year in the military near Orleans, Gaston would drive him to the station at the end of each leave, even accompanying him on the train as far as Orleans itself, only to turn around and go right back to Paris. According to Pouquet, Gaston invited Proust to be his best man for their wedding.

Pouquet's mother-in-law, Madame Arman de Caillavet (née Léontine Lippmann), held one of the most important salons of the time at her home in 12, avenue Hoche. The featured "regular" was Anatole France, who was one of the most important novelists of the period—he was awarded the Nobel Prize for Literature in 1921—and one of the models for the writer Bergotte in RTP; more than likely he was also Léontine's lover. At Madame Arman de Caillevet's urging, France provided an introduction to Proust's first book, *Les Plaisirs et les jours* (she often wrote brief pieces under France's name, however, and may have written the introduction to Proust's book herself). In gratitude, Proust inscribed a copy of the book to her, quoting lines from France's *La Vie littéraire*.

Around the turn of the century, Gaston Arman de Caillavet became well known as a writer of light comedies and later produced several very popular works with another of Proust's friends, Robert de Flers (1872–1927), before he died at the age of forty-five. Jeanne Arman de Caillavet later married her cousin Maurice and regained the name Pouquet. She also produced a history of her first mother-in-law's salon, *Le Salon de Madame Arman de Caillavet*, which included charming memories of Proust and France, among others. Pouquet's daughter with Arman de Caillavet, Simone, was thought to be one of the models for the daughter of Gilberte Swann and Robert de Saint-Loup in RTP, Mademoiselle de Saint-Loup, who appears in the last section of the book. Simone Arman de Caillavet later married André Maurois, Proust's biographer.

There is a particularly poignant (albeit unreferenced) anecdote about Pouquet in Philippe Julian's mordant biography of the poet Robert de Montesquiou, who is often cited as a model for the Baron de Charlus in RTP. It seems that for years Pouquet, thinking that she and Montesquiou had an affectionate relationship, wrote him warm letters. In 1921, when Montesquiou died, one of his few bequests was a small *coffret* to Madame Pouquet. It was duly delivered, and when she raised its lid, she discovered all her letters. Not a single one had been opened.

A translation of this poem can also be found in Gerard Hopkins's English version of André Maurois's biography *Proust: Portrait of a Genius*.

POEM 9
Translated by Deborah Treisman

Most likely written during the same period as Poem 6, when Proust was "courting" Laure de Chevigné (see notes to that poem), because of the reference to her "bird-like" appearance. Proust once wrote to his friend Armand de Gramont, then the duc de Guiche (only later did he attain the title of duc de Gramont) that the duchesse de Guermantes "resembles a tough barnyard fowl whom I formerly took to be a bird of paradise. By transforming her into a puissant vulture, I have at least prevented the public assuming that she was just a commonplace old magpie." (Translation of this letter by Marcel Schneider.) Interestingly, the caricaturist SEM (Georges Goursat, 1863–1934) once depicted Proust's friends poet Anna de Noailles and producer Gabriel Astruc as birds.

Poems 10 to 16

Poems 10 to 16 are usually considered to show the influence of Charles Baudelaire (1821–1867), arguably Proust's favorite poet, about whom he wrote two essays, including one published in 1921 in which he supposedly, and often incorrectly, quoted Baudelaire's poems from memory. In his adolescence and early adulthood Proust was also influenced by Paul Verlaine (1844–1896), Alfred de Musset (1810–1857), and Gérard de Nerval (né Gérard Labrunie, 1808–1855), about whom he wrote a brief appreciation that Bernard de Fallois included in the 1954 version of Proust's draft work that Fallois titled *Contre Saint-Beuve*. They were probably written in 1890 and 1891.

POEM 10
Translated by Deborah Treisman

Written on the reverse of a letter that appears to have been written when Proust was performing his military service in 1890.

POEM 11
Translated by Susan Stewart

POEM 12
Translated by Deborah Treisman

POEM 13
Translated by Deborah Treisman

POEM 14
Translated by Jennifer Moxley

POEM 15
Translated by Meena Alexander

Appears to have been written in 1891 while Proust was staying with his friends the Baignières at their Normandy home, Les Frémonts, Trouville, Calvados, which was written on the reverse side of the page.

POEM 16
Translated by Mark Polizzotti

Poems 17 to 25: *Les Plaisirs et les jours* (Pleasures and Days)

In May 1894, at the Paris salon of painter Madeleine Lemaire (1845–1928; see Poem 80 and its notes), Proust was introduced to the young composer Reynaldo Hahn (1874–1947), two and a half years his junior (Hahn's date of birth has been reported as both 1874 and 1875). Their immediate rapport grew during their twenty-eight-year relationship, which ended only with Proust's death in 1922. Within days of this meeting, the two decided to collaborate. They spent time together at Madeleine Lemaire's country house east of Paris in Réveillon and traveled frequently in one another's company. For more information on Hahn, see the section "Poèmes à . . . /Poems to."

Les Plaisirs et les jours (the original title echoes Hesiod's *Works and Days* [*Erga kai Hēmérai*], but translated by Louise Varese in 1948 as *Pleasures and Regrets* and published without its poems, it may reflect a bit of Proust's interest in Ralph Waldo Emerson) included an introduction by Anatole France, the pre-eminent novelist of his time who, in 1921, would receive the Nobel Prize for Literature, and illustrations by Lemaire, an artist best known for her flower paintings. The inclusion of artwork in this type of publication was not unusual, and most likely Proust got the idea from the publication of Robert de Montesquiou's *Les Chauves-Souris* (The Bats, 1892), which included illustrations by James Abbott McNeill Whistler, Antonio de La Gandara, Jean-Louis Forain, and Yamamoto. Proust's volume, measuring 11.5 inches by 8 inches, was expensive (13.50 francs, at a time when first works of fiction would sell for a couple of francs) and, according to Robert Dreyfus, Proust's friends made fun of what seemed at the time like a frivolous venture, in a skit published in their magazine *Le Banquet* (Note: Ernest La Jeunesse, 1874–1917, and Fernand Gregh, 1873–1960):

Proust, addressing Ernest La Jeunesse: Have you read my book?

La Jeunesse: No, sir, it's too expensive.

Proust: Alas, that's what everyone is telling me . . . and you, Gregh, have you read it?

Gregh: Yes, I divided it up, so I could justify it.

Proust: And did you find it too expensive, too?

Gregh: Not at all. I got my money's worth.

Proust: For sure. A preface by Anatole France, 4 francs . . . pictures by Madame Lemaire, 4 francs . . . music by Reynaldo Hahn, 4 francs . . . my prose, one franc . . . a few of my poems, 50 centimes . . . so that makes thirteen-fifty . . . not really an overly large amount, eh?

La Jeunesse: But, sir, there are a great deal more things in the *Hachette Almanac*, and that costs only 25 sous!

Proust (laughing):   That's too funny! Oh, it hurts me to laugh so much . . . It must be very amusing to be so witty.

Poems 17 to 21: Portraits of Painters

Included in *Les Plaisirs et les jours* were four poems Proust based on favored painters Albert Cuyp, Paulus Potter, Anton Van Dyck, and Antoine Watteau, which Hahn set to music. Flemish and Dutch art was important to Proust, who had grown up with reproductions of these paintings on the walls of his home. In 1902, in the company of his friend Bertrand de Fénelon, Proust traveled to Holland and Belgium (including Dordrecht, see poems 36 and 37) to see Dutch and Flemish paintings.

According to critic Theodore Johnson Jr., Proust was inspired by the tradition of ekphrasis, popularized in the nineteenth century by such poets as Verlaine and Baudelaire ("Les Phares" comes immediately to mind). But they—and the following portraits of musicians—also anticipate Proust's interest in the integration of the various fine arts—writing, painting, and music—which receives much deeper treatment in RTP with the portraits of the fictional writer Bergotte, the painter Elstir, and the composer Vinteuil. Proust also wrote an essay on the painters Rembrandt and Chardin, which reveal his burgeoning belief and growing aesthetic principle that the artist's ability to transform the most quotidian of subjects into art is central to his genius. The "Portraits of Painters" were read, played, and performed several times in private homes and public forums. Proust read them to Colette, who chided him for denigrating his own work. In April 1895, Proust sought to have them published in the journal *La Revue de Paris*, but they were rejected by editor Jean-Louis Ganderax. They appeared in *Le Gaulois* on June 21, 1895, and in the book *L'Année des poètes* (The Year in Poetry, 1895). In 1896, the "Portraits" were published in Proust's first book, *Les Plaisirs et les jours*. They also appeared, with Hahn's sheet music, from the music publisher Menestrel, with a dedication to the poet José María de Heredia.

POEMS 17 AND 18
Translated by Richard Howard

Tadié notes that these two poems were based on the painting *Départ pour la promenade* (*Departure for a Promenade*) by Albert Cuyp (1620–1691) in the collection of the Louvre Museum, Paris. Cuyp was born and died in Dordrecht, which Proust would visit in 1902, in the company of his friend Bertrand de Fénelon (see also poems 36 and 37 and notes to Poem 36). The second version was found in manuscript. Because it was included in the *Cahier*, we have included it here.

POEM 19
Translated by Richard Howard

Based on the painting *Deux chevaux de trait devant une chaumière* (*Two Workhorses in Front of a Thatch-roofed Cottage*) by Paulus Potter (1625–1654) in the Louvre Museum, Paris. Proust had read *Les maîtres d'autrefois* (The Masters of Yesteryear) by Eugène Fromentin (1820–1876), published in 1876, in which the painter and critic Fromentin expressed his admiration for Potter. Proust took *Les maîtres* with him on his 1902 tour of the Low Countries. See also Poem 101 for Proust's rerendering of this poem, dedicated to his housekeeper, Céleste Albaret.

POEM 20

Translated by Richard Howard

Based on *L'embarquement pour Cythère* (*The Embarcation for Cythera*), a *fête galante* painting by Jean-Antoine Watteau (1684–1721) in the Louvre Museum, Paris. The isle of Cythera and Watteau's painting about it were frequent topics in the eighteenth and nineteenth centuries and included in works by Proust's favorite poets: Baudelaire, Nerval, and Verlaine. Nerval in particular must have inspired Proust's interest in this painting. In the section of his *Sylvie* called "Un Voyage à Cythère" there is "La traversée du lac avait été imaginée peut-être pour rappeler le *Voyage à Cythère* de Watteau" (The lake-crossing was created perhaps to remind one of Watteau's *Voyage to Cythera*). In *Cahiers Marcel Proust n. 1* "Hommage à Marcel Proust," Jacques Truelle quotes Proust as telling him "Never has a book moved me as much as Gérard de Nerval's *Sylvie*." ("Jamais livre ne m'a autant ému que *Sylvie* de Gérard de Nerval.") For more information on Proust and Watteau, see his essay reprinted in *Essais et articles*.

POEM 21

Translated by Richard Howard

Based on a portrait then identified as the Duke of Richmond in the Louvre by Anthony (Anton) van Dyck (1599–1641), it was later revealed that James Richmond was not born until forty years later.

Poems 22 to 25: Portraits of Musicians

In 1895, Proust asked his friend Léon Daudet, who worked for the *Nouvelle Revue Française*, to try to get these four poems published in that journal, without success (see Proust's letter to Lucien Daudet of October 7, 1895). At the time, the NRF was edited by Juliette Adam (1836–1936), with whom Proust had an uneasy relationship. The poems would receive their first publication in *Les Plaisirs et les jours*.

Proust's interest in music was enhanced not only by his friendship with Hahn but by his growing relationship with the Prince and Princesse Edmond de Polignac, the former a composer, the latter (née Winnaretta Singer) a painter. Not only were both Polignacs highly regarded as artists, they were important patrons, as well. Their salon brought together some of the most important new composers of the time, include Gabriel Fauré, Maurice Ravel, and Vincent D'Indy, and the princesse, in particular, amassed a significant collection of impressionist painting. For more information on Proust's take on the salon, see his essay "Le Salon de Prince Edmond de Polignac," published in *Le Figaro* on September 6, 1903, signed with Proust's Shakespearean pen name, Horatio (it is reprinted in *Essais et articles*). Its appearance created tension between him and the princesse.

POEM 22

Translated by Richard Howard

Frederic Chopin (1810–1849) was one of the foremost composers of the first half of the nineteenth century. According to P. F. Prestwich's *The Translation of Memories*, at one point early on when Proust and Hahn met they thought about jointly writing a biography of Chopin. In RTP, Chopin appears most prominently in a discussion of his work by the seaside. This poem was dedicated to the pianist Édouard Risler (1873–1929), a close friend of Reynaldo Hahn who specialized in the music of Chopin, touring Europe and playing the composer's complete works.

POEM 23

Translated by Lauren Watel

Christopher Willibald Gluck (1714–1787) was an opera composer born in Germany who spent much of his professional career in Vienna and Paris. The references to Hercules, Armida, Admetus, Iphigenia, Orpheus, and Alcestis refer to characters in his operas *Armide, Iphigenia in Tauris, Iphigenia in Aulis, Alceste,* and *Orfeo et Euridice.* For information on Watteau, see note to Poem 20.

Line 14   The River Styx formed the border of the Greek underworld.

POEM 24

Translated by Lauren Watel

Robert Schumann (1810–1856) was a German composer of the Romantic period. The reference to carnival in line 8 is to his "Carnaval," in which Schumann attempted to fuse the literary and musical.

POEM 25

Translated by Lauren Watel

Wolfgang Amadeus Mozart (1756–1791). At the age of thirteen, when asked for his favorite composer in the famous questionnaire, Proust answered "Mozart." This poem mainly refers to Mozart's operas.

Line 9   Cherubino appears in *The Marriage of Figaro*,
                Don Juan in *Don Giovanni*.

Line 16   Reference to the opera *The Magic Flute*.

Poems 26–27: Two Prose Poems

POEM 26
Translated by Lydia Davis

Jacques Bizet (1872–1922) was Proust's schoolmate at the Lycée Condorcet. His father was the composer Georges Bizet, whose works included the opera *Carmen*. His mother was Geneviève Halévy, daughter of Fromentin Halévy, composer of the opera *La Juive*, which features prominently in RTP (see notes to poems 1 and 3). She later married businessman Émile Straus. She and Proust became very close and shared an inclination toward neurasthenia. (Élisabeth de Gramont wrote that they "had the same ravaged nervous system.") Proust used her and her salon as source material for the character and salon of Madame Verdurin in RTP.

Jacques Bizet was a very, very close friend (supposedly, Proust, at the age of fifteen or sixteen, suggested a homosexual affair to him but was refused). Bizet committed suicide two weeks before Proust's death in 1922.

Poems 26 and 27 were composed for the *Revue Lilas*, a schoolboy journal produced in November 1888 (when Proust was seventeen; hence, the second part of number 26). In his biography, William Carter says that "[t]hese are the first writings in which Marcel consciously fictionalizes his own voice in the first person." There are echoes of the opening of *À la recherche du temps perdu* in Poem 26, but the poem is decidedly immature compared RTP.

POEM 27
Translated by Lydia Davis

At the end of this prose poem Proust noted "H. Heine trad. M.P." An endnote in the Francis and Gontier collection says that "this piece was translated from a German version at the Lycée Condorcet." Fortini omits it from his Italian translation because "it seems to be a translation from Heine." I have not been able to locate anything in Heine that approximates it.

POEM 28
Translated by Meena Alexander

Written on the reserve side of the envelope of a letter that Proust's father sent from Aix-en-Provence on October 9, 1889.

Line 2   Yuldo is a Korean utopia.

POEM 29
Translated by Jennifer Moxley

Written on one of the pages Proust's mother sent to him on "mourning" (black-bordered) stationery. Proust's paternal grandmother, Virginie Proust, had died on March 19, 1889. In September, Proust spent some time at the family home of his friend Horace Finaly.

POEM 30
Translated by Jennifer Moxley

Line 1   Marie de Rabutin-Chantal, marquise de Sévigné (1626–1696) is best known for the hundreds of loving letters she wrote to her daughter, Françoise, over several decades in the seventeenth century. In RTP, Madame de Sévigné's letters are regularly quoted by the narrator's mother and grandmother; the latter gives him a volume of the letters to read on the train to Balbec. Sevigné's Hôtel Carnavalet in the Marais section of Paris now houses a museum devoted to Parisian history, the Musée Carnavalet. It includes an exhibition of Proust's bedroom furniture as well as Anna de Noailles's sitting-room furniture.

The duc de Saint-Simon (1675–1755) is considered to be the most important memoirist in French history, whose style influenced Proust's fictional autobiography, *À la recherche du temps perdu*. Proust wrote a hilarious pastiche of Saint-Simon (published in *Pastiches et mélanges*) in which he said that many British people thought that Elizabeth Asquith, who had married Proust's great friend Antoine Bibesco, "could have done better."

Voltaire (François Marie Arouet, 1694–1778) was one of the most important writers and philosophers of the French Enlightenment. He is mentioned several times by various characters in RTP. Reynaldo Hahn named his basset hound after one of Voltaire's characters, Zadig (see the notes to Poem 57).

Line 5   Joseph Joubert (1754–1824), French philosopher
          who believed that his own invalidism contributed
          to wisdom in his thinking and is best known for
          his *Pensées*. In the introduction to a collection of
          Proust's letters to Georges de Lauris, *À un ami*,
          Lauris notes that "Marcel had an infinite liking
          for Joubert. Like himself, Joubert had been an in-
          valid. Like himself, he had expected to leave no
          legacy of his ideas, extensive and subtle though
          they were. But behind his own weakness, as be-
          hind that of Joubert, there was strength, as would
          one day be clear . . ." See Proust's essay on Joubert
          in *Essais et articles*.

Line 8   Ximénès Doudan (1800–1872) was a French jour-
(7 in the nalist who once wrote, "Everything without tells
French)   the individual that he is nothing; everything
          within persuades him that he is everything."

          Gaius Plinius Secundus, known as Pliny the Elder
          (23–79), was the author of *Natural History* and a
          twenty-volume work, *The History of the German
          Wars*.

          Honoré de Balzac (1799–1850) was one of the
          foremost writers in France in the first half of
          the nineteenth century and produced over 100
          novels primarily gathered under the rubric of *La
          Comédie humaine* (*The Human Comedy*). He was
          a particular favorite of Proust and had great influ-
          ence on the "panorama" structure of RTP. For
          more information on Proust and Balzac, see Wal-
          ter A. Strauss's *Proust and Literature*, Margaret
          Mein's *A Foretaste of Proust*, and Anka Muhl-
          stein's *Monsieur Proust's Library*.

POEM 31

Translated by Meena Alexander

POEM 32

Translated by Wayne Koestenbaum

Lies (*mensonges*) are a continuing theme in all of Proust's work, from this poem, composed in the early 1890s and set to music by Proust's friend Léon Delafosse, to the withholding of truth in various stories in *Les Plaisirs et les jours*, to the many and varied subterfuges (and outright lying) that take place throughout RTP. In RTP, the narrator notes that "lying is essential to humanity. Lying may play as big a role as the search for pleasure, and is even ordered about by that search. You lie to protect your pleasure, or your honor, if the revelation of that pleasure runs contrary to honor. We lie all our lives, even, especially perhaps, only to those who love us. Indeed, only they make us fear for our pleasure and make us long for their esteem." It's also possible that when writing, Proust was thinking of Baudelaire's poem "L'amour du mensonge."

The poem and Delafosse's music were published by Menestrel in 1895 and included in "Six Poems by Bourget, Proust, Pierre Quillant, Marceline, Desbordes-Valmore, Montesquiou." The former was also reproduced in Alec Ralph Hobson's *A Tribute to the Memory of a Friend* (London, 1925) as "Sur des yeux" (About Your Eyes) without any reference to its musical setting. There is also a longer version available in Philip Kolb's *Textes retrouvés*.

POEM 33

Translated by Wayne Koestenbaum

This poem also appeared in Hobson (see note to Poem 32), with slight variations in lines 5 and 8.

POEM 34
Translated by Anna Moschovakis

In 1902, after the death of his mother, Antoine Bibesco returned to Romania to administer the Bibesco estates. Proust contemplated joining him there and even planned to do so, until two obstacles kept him from it. One was the wedding of Proust's brother, Robert, in early February (moved up from March). Robert was to marry Marthe Dubois-Amiot, the daughter of a woman with whom their father, Adrien, had had a close relationship. On the day of the wedding, both Proust and his mother took ill: Proust arrived swaddled in several overcoats and his usual cotton stuffing. He spent the following three days in bed. Mme Proust arrived in an ambulance.

The second obstacle had to do with Proust's own health. According to Marthe Bibesco, in her 1948 memoir *Au Bal avec Marcel Proust* (*Marcel Proust at the Ball*) when Proust learned from Bibesco that the fruit trees would be blossoming at the time he would be there, he was compelled to cancel his trip. To an asthmatic, flowering fruit trees would have made any stay there untenable. The poem was reproduced in Marthe Bibesco's book. See Poem 88 and its notes for more information on Proust's relationship with Marthe Bibesco, and poems 84 and 87 regarding Antoine Bibesco.

POEM 35
Translated by Susan Stewart

POEM 36
Translated by Meena Alexander

The Dordrecht poems (numbers 36 and 37) were written in October 1902, when Proust and Bertrand de Fénelon traveled to the Low Countries to see the art; Proust sent the poems to Reynaldo

Hahn, along with a drawing. Proust went to the top of the church tower "to enjoy the panoramic views," according to William Carter, and sent a twenty-seven-line poem to Reynaldo Hahn, which Tadié calls "a pastiche of Baudelaire, Verlaine, and Musset."

Note: Albert Cuyp was born in Dordrecht (see Poem 17 and its note).

POEM 37

Translated by Meena Alexander

See notes to Poem 36 above.

POEM 38

Translated by Jeff Clark

Line 2   Refers to the painter Madeleine Lemaire's "at-homes," when she and her daughter Suzette would receive people (interesting that Proust would focus on Wednesdays when Lemaire's salons took place on Tuesday). See the introduction to "Portraits of Painters" for more information on Lemaire and Poem 80 and its notes.

Line 3   Painter James Abbott McNeill Whistler (1834–1903) was one of the models for the painter Elstir in RTP. His portrait of Montesquiou, known as *Arrangement in Black and Gold: Comte Robert de Montesquiou-Fézensac*, was painted in 1891–92. He and Proust met at least once and a copy of

Whistler's portrait of Thomas Carlyle hung in Proust's bedroom.

Michelangelo di Lodovico Buonarroti Simoni (1475–1564), the Italian Renaissance painter and sculptor.

Francisco Goya (1746–1828), the Spanish romantic painter.

Line 9   The syrinx was a reed instrument, like pan pipes. A mirliton is generally a type of reed pipe or kazoo. See also Poem 98.

Line 10   Gaston most likely refers to Gaston Arman de Caillavet (see notes to Poem 8).

Line 12   Germiny most likely refers to Jacques LeBègue de Germiny (1872–1950).

Charles-Etienne-Louis Ganderax (1855–1940) was the founder and editor of the *Revue de Paris*. Proust created the adjective "ganderesque" from his last name (see Proust's *Carnets*).

Brinquand may refer to Vincent Brinquant, father of the future wife of the duc de Polignac.

Line 14   Suzette was Madeleine Lemaire's daughter, who was known as "La Jeune Veuve" ("The Young Widow"; her mother was known as "The Widow"). She had a reputation for being cold.

POEM 39

Translated by Wyatt Mason

POEM 40

Translated by Harold Augenbraum

Nicolas Cottin (1873–1916) was a servant in the Proust family household and, after the death of Proust's parents, from 1907 to 1914—when he left to fight in World War I—Proust's own, along with his housekeeper-wife Céline (though she was sacked for being a busybody, according to Céleste Albaret). He died of pleurisy in 1916.

The importance of coffee service dated back to when Proust's parents were alive. According to Céleste, who draws a vivid portrait of such rituals, the household always bought its coffee at Corcellet's in the rue de Lévis, where Mme Proust had bought hers, because that was where it was roasted and hence was freshest: the Corcellet family had been selling coffee since 1760. The servants would prepare the "morning" coffee for early afternoon, when Proust generally awoke and rang for it. One always waited for the ring, and the coffee had to be ready. They placed one croissant on the tray, though they always bought two, in case he wanted a second with his second cup, though his eating both was rare. The legend of Proust as a coffee drinker derives from his belief that many cups of coffee a day could assuage, and perhaps even prevent, an asthma attack. He was thought to have drunk as many as twenty cups a day.

POEM 41
Translated by Wyatt Mason

This poem was written in early October, 1911, as Proust entered the period of intense writing of RTP.

Line 2   Paul Bourget (1852–1935) was one of the foremost novelists of the time who, by the end of the century, had become an anti-Dreyfusard (and hence, not high in Proust's estimation). Among his novels was the brief novel *Gladys Harvey* (1888), based on the life of Proust's great-uncle Louis's mistress Laure Hayman. See notes to Poem 2 for more information.

Line 3   Proust had a more complicated artistic relationship with René Boylesve (1867–1926). In his essay in *Cahiers Marcel Proust n. 1, Hommage à Marcel Proust,* Boylesve wrote that at first he had an unfavorable impression of Proust's work but later changed his mind. According to Laurent Lesage's *Literary Friendships of Marcel Proust,* Boylesve "once declared bitterly that Proust had accomplished what he himself had always dreamed of."

POEM 42
Translated by Mary Ann Caws

Anna de Noailles (née Anna Elisabeth Bibesco-Bassaraba de Brancvan, 1876–1933) was one of the foremost poets of her day. She produced over twenty books of poetry, memoir, and fiction. Proust admired her work greatly.

Line 4   Nice is a city on the Côte d'Azur. Yeddo is an alternate name for Tokyo. Anna de Noailles refers to it in her poem "L'offrande."

                J'ai vu des îles d'or aux temples parfumés,
                Et ce Yeddo, plein de voix frêles de mousmés.

Line 6   Katsushika Hokusai (1760–1849) was a Japanese artist and printmaker of the Edo period whose work influenced many European artists of the nineteenth century.

Line 8   Le Vésinet was a wooded district to the west of Paris visited by many notables of the mid- and late nineteenth century, including Bizet, Degas, Montesquiou, and Apollinaire. It is close to Le Pecq (see the following line). For more information, see Sophie Cueille, *Le Vésinet: Modèle français d'urbanisme paysager, 1858–1930.*

Line 10   Mount Valérien is a hill where a fortress of the same name is located, just west of the Bois de Boulogne. The fortress has also been used as a prison.

Line 12   "In the Champs-de-Mars, there used to be a large paddle-wheel. Artesian wells of Passy were at the corner of Lamartine Square and l'avenue Henri Martin." Note by Francis and Gontier.

POEM 43

Translated by Anna Moschovakis

The poet Stéphane Mallarmé (1842–1898) published a series of "address" poems, "Addresses or the Postman's Leisure." Proust had an uneven relationship with Mallarmé, particularly after the former published the essay "Contre l'obscurité" (Against Obscurity), which criticized symbolist poetry and to which Mallarmé later responded in public.

Line 3   The poet Anna de Noailles (see notes to Poem 42).

Line 9   The "Widow" was Madeleine Lemaire. See notes to Poem 80.

Line 12   La Fitz-James was the Comtesse Robert de Fitz-James (née Rosalie von Gutmann, 1862–1923). For a warm appreciation of her and her salon, see Edith Wharton's *A Backward Glance.*

Line 17   La Chevigné is the Comtesse Adhéaume de Chevigné (née Laure de Sade, 1859–1936). For more information, see note to Poem 6. Jean Cocteau also lived at this address.

Line 20   Marcel Proust lived at 102, boulevard Haussmann from late 1906 to 1919.

Line 21   For information on Laure Hayman, see note to Poem 2.

Line 23   Proust's friend Marie Scheikévitch (1882–1965?) married and subsequently divorced Pierre Carolus-Duran, son of the painter Charles Carolus-Duran (1837–1917). In her memoir, *Souvenirs d'un temps disparu* (*Time Past*), she notes that in 1917 Proust attended a dinner at her home with her sister-in-law, "Madame Hellmann, daughter of Carolus-Duran, who, like myself, lived at the Trianon Palace Hotel."

Line 25   For information on Lilli Lehmann, see note to
           Poem 50.

Line 27   Édouard Hermann (1865–1932) was a musician
           friend of Hahn. In a letter Kolb dated November
           12 or 13, 1915, Proust notes that Hermann played
           Hahn's four-handed waltzes with Hahn at a musi-
           cale at the home of Mme Duglé.

POEM 44
Translated by Marcella Durand and Michel Durand

Robert de Montesquiou-Fézensac (1855–1921) was a well-known
poet of the day, friend of Oscar Wilde, the model for the deca-
dent character des Esseintes in Joris-Karl Huysmans's *À rebours*,
and one of the models for the Baron de Charlus in RTP. His
1892 collection of poetry was an inspiration for Proust's *Les
Plaisirs et les jours* (unfortunately so, according to Tadié). He
was considered one of the great aesthetes of the time, a dandy,
and a snob. He was sixteen years older than Proust, and their
relationship was always fraught. It began with Proust's typical
toadying address and ended with Montesquiou's sniffing irrita-
tion at being portrayed so abominably in RTP (see Elisabeth de
Gramont's portrait of their friendship in *Robert de Montes-
quiou and Marcel Proust: An Intimate Friendship*). He was the
subject of portraits by James Abbott McNeill Whistler (see note
to Poem 38) and Giovanni Boldini, in which he drips with arro-
gance, but when painted by Philip de László he appears stern
and serious.

   They met in the spring of 1893 at the home of Madeleine Le-
maire. Later Proust would write to him, "As a matter of fact the
pastiche that would most amuse me to do when I can write a bit
(without prejudice to more serious studies) is one of you! But in
the first place it would probably annoy you, and I don't want
anything of mine to annoy you. I'm too fond of you for that, and
secondly I feel that I should never be able to, never know how

to!" See the last paragraph of the note to Poem 8 for more information on Montesquiou.

Dedication — Aimé François Philibert, marquis, then duc de Clermont-Tonnerre (1871–1940). He married Elisabeth de Gramont, the half sister of Proust's great friend the duc de Guiche.

Line 2 — Paros is an island in the Aegean Sea where pure white marble was quarried in the classical period. Carrara is a town and quarry in Tuscany from which the great Renaissance sculptors, including Michaelangelo, drew their marble.

Line 4 — Hardy-Tea is a hybrid rose.

Line 6 — Cloton was the nickname of Mme Gaston Legrand, née Clotilde de Fournès. According to Antoine Compagnon in his notes to *Sodome et Gomorrhe*, who cites a 1922 letter from Proust to Robert de Flers, she was a model for Mme d'Orvillers in RTP.

Line 7 — In 1906, Montesquiou acquired the Palais Rose in Le Vésinet (see notes to Poem 42), which resembled the Grand Trianon in Versailles and was built around the turn of the century for the engineer Arthur Schweizer. It should not be confused with the Palais Rose of Boni de Castellane on the avenue Foch in Paris, whose façade was also based on the Grand Trianon.

Vézelay most likely refers to the Church of the Madeleine at Vézelay. Proust visited there in September 1903 and found the church to be "as much like a Turkish bath as it does like Notre-Dame."

Line 8   The Clermont-Tonnerres lived at 74, rue Lauriston.

Line 12   The duc of Clermont-Tonnerre received the château of Glissolles upon his marriage to Elisabeth de Gramont. At the time of the writing of this poem, he was also mayor of Glissolles (in Proust's original, Glissolles is spelled with a single "s"). Clermont-Tonnerre also owned the Château d'Ancy-le-franc.

POEM 45
Translated by Anna Moschovakis

A pastiche of Debussy's opera *Pelléas et Mélisande*, this dialogue was written in February 1911. The name Markel is a conflation of Marcel and Arkel, one of the main characters in the opera.

Poems 46 to 54: Vers Burlesques et Satiriques

POEM 46
Translated by Wyatt Mason

Most likely written during the first semester of 1892, when Proust, Jean Boissonnas, and Robert de Billy took a course with Albert Vandal.

In 1891, Proust enrolled in the École Libre de sciences-politiques (known later as "Sciences-Po") to study philosophy. One of the foremost professors there was Albert Vandal (1853–1910) who gave a course in "oriental matters." Vandal was a prominent scholar whose major works included the prizewinning three-volume *Napoleon and Alexander I*.

In this poem, which was scrawled on the back of an envelope, Proust mentions three of his schoolmates: Gabriel Trarieux (1870–1940), with whom Proust would collaborate on the short-lived magazine *Le Banquet* and who later would become a well-known novelist, poet, playwright, and editor (Tadié dismisses the young Trarieux by saying he was a "self-styled innovator"); Robert de Billy (1869–1953), who would become a diplomat (see Poems 78 and 79 and their notes); and Jean Boissonnas (1870–1953), to whom Proust addressed Poem 104.

POEM 47
Translated by Jeff Clark

Line 2   Béatrice most likely refers to Charlotte Béatrice de Rothschild (1864–1934), a member of the prominent banking family. In 1883, she married Maurice Ephrussi, whose cousin Charles Ephrussi was an art connoisseur and is thought to be one of the models for Charles Swann in RTP. In *Pays Parisiens*, Daniel Halévy suggests that Ephrussi would have been better inspiration than Haas, although Halévy also thought that Albert Cavé would have made a better model than either of the Charleses.

Gustava was the pet name for Cécile Anspach, Lady Gustave de Rothschild (1840–1912), who was, according to historian Niall Ferguson, one of the first "Jewish outsiders" to marry into that family. Daughter of attorney Philippe Anspach, honorary advocate in the Cour de cassation, Cécile married the handsome (according to Constance Battersea's memoirs) heir to the banking fortune and gave birth to three daughters and three sons. She was Proust's distant cousin by marriage—Albert Berncastel, the brother of Proust's great-great-grandfather on his mother's side, Nathan Berncastel, married Sarah Anspach;

Cécile was Sarah's uncle's granddaughter. Lady Rothschild also appears as Gustava in poems 63, line 12, and 70, line 9.

Line 3   André Chaumeix (1874–1955) was a French critic. For the last three decades of his life he would maintain a liaison with the writer María de Regnier, daughter of poet José María de Heredia and wife of poet Henri de Regnier.

Henry de Jouvenel des Ursin (1876–1935) was the editor of the daily *Le Matin* when he became the author Colette's second husband. They separated when she began an affair with his son from his first marriage to Claire Boas, Bertrand (hence, Colette's stepson).

Although Proust knew future French prime minister Léon Blum (1872–1950) when they were in their late teens and they worked on the *Revue Blanche* together, this probably refers to his younger brother René (1878–1943), who helped negotiate Proust's publishing contract for *Du côté de chez Swann* (*Swann's Way*) with publisher Bernard Grasset and was instrumental in bringing the Ballets Russes to France (see Judith Chazin-Bennahum's *René Blum and the Ballets Russes*).

Line 4   The Château de Courances is located in Essonne about twenty-five miles south of Paris.

According to Kolb, Proust got his information on the Château de Verteuil from Saint-Simon's *Memoirs*. It is located about forty miles northeast of Cognac in southwest France.

Nonelef was the anagrammatic pet name for Bertrand de Salignac-Fénelon (1878–1914), who was one of the models for Robert de St. Loup in RTP. Transposition of the letters of friends' family names was typical jokestering on the part of Proust and his friends (e.g., Bibesco and his family were often known as "the Ocsebibs"). William Carter's biography notes that Fénelon was Louisa de Mornand's lover before she was Albufera's and there is a notation in Proust's 1908 notebook that Fénelon was the lover of Louisa de Mornand's sister, Suzanne. Fénelon was killed in World War I.

POEM 48

Translated by Marcella Durand and Michel Durand

Sent to Reynaldo Hahn in the fall of 1907. The ellipses refer to places where Proust ripped off pieces of the page to hide the name of the person referred.

Line 3 Nicholas Lancret (1690–1743) was a French painter who specialized in "soft-focus" portraits and scenes of upper-class and aristocratic women (who were highly powdered) and *fêtes galantes* paintings. In this particular case, the "speckling" ("soupoudre" in line 6) may refer to the use of face powder to hide blemishes in her skin, since in the eighteenth century face powder was used to hid pocks created by a bout with smallpox.

Line 11 Kolb suggests Thérésa refers to Mme Emma Valladon (1837–1913), a well-known cabaret singer whose stage name was Thérésa. Thérésa was known as a vulgarian. See Juliette Adam, *Mes sentiments et nos idées avant 1870.*

POEM 49
Translated by Wyatt Mason

This poem was written between August 6 and 9, 1906, and included in a letter to Reynaldo Hahn. At the end of the letter, Proust asks Hahn to burn both poem and letter. Proust was living alone in the Hôtel des Réservoirs in Versailles at the time (the former Hôtel de Madame de Pompadour) while the apartment in a building owned by the Proust brothers and their aunt Amélie, his Uncle Georges's widow, at 102, boulevard Haussmann was being renovated for his use. The brothers sold their shares to Aunt Amélie in 1908, but Proust continued living there until she sold the building in 1919 to a banker and Proust was forced to leave. A bank still occupies the first floor.

Line 4   Lucienne Bréval was born Bertha Agnès Lisette Schilling in Zurich in 1869 and died in Neuilly-sur-Seine in 1935. She may have taken her name to associate her career with the composer Jean Baptiste Bréval. Lucienne Bréval was a barrel-chested soprano who performed mostly with the Opera National de Paris between 1892 and 1919, specializing in French grand opera and Wagner's heroines (a critic once compared her onstage as Brünnhilde to "a rock lobster"). Her repertoire included roles in Meyerbeer's *Les Huguenots* and Wagner's *Die Walküre*. In 1902, she began an affair with Proust's friend Antoine Bibesco (the "A.B." of line 10 in the poem). The relationship lasted several passionate years, throughout which Bibesco's friends described him as star-struck. Proust not only wrote to Hahn about it, but added in a postscript to a letter to Georges de Lauris that "I hear that Mademoiselle B. is inconsolable at Antoine's departure" (interestingly, in the same letter he quotes the lines he used as an epigraph to Poem 6; see the notes to Poem 6). In a letter to director Bibesco's Lycée Condorcet schoolmate and close friend Jacques Copeau (1879–1949), writer André Gide (1869–1951) noted that Bibesco had gone to the United States, "fleeing (Bréval's) Wagnerian embrace," (see André Gide and Jacques Copeau, *Correspondance*). In the letter of August 9, 1906, in which the poem was enclosed, Proust noted that Bibesco was in San Francisco. His Valkyrie remained in France. For more information on Antoine Bibesco, see the note to Poem 84.

Line 11   Son of novelist Alphonse Daudet and an author in his own right, according to Kate Cambor's *Gilded Youth*, Léon Daudet (1867–1942) had an affair with Lucienne Bréval. Proust dedicated *The Guermantes Way* to him.

According to Theodore Zeldin's *A History of French Passions, 1848–1945: Intellect, Taste, and Anxiety*, Eugène Lautier (1867–1935) was "a large fat man, a bachelor with an enormous appetite, whose favorite saying was 'I was never wrong.'" From 1905 to 1909, he directed the *Figaro*'s foreign affairs service, where Proust met him. He later became undersecretary of fine arts for France.

A friend of Proust, Pol Louis Neveux (1865–1939) was a novelist (among his works is the novel *Golo*) and inspector of libraries.

Philip Kolb speculates that this refers to Georges Leygues (1857–1933), who was minister of public instruction and fine arts, and who served as prime minister of France 1910–21.

Line 12   The chaste author of *Ferval* refers to Vincent
          d'Indy (1851–1931), a composer and director of
          the Schola Cantorum.

Line 13   Music critic of *Le Temps*, Pierre Lalo (1866–1943)
          was the son of composer Édouard Lalo. Fauré's
          Nocturne no. 11 in F# minor, op. 104/1 (1913) was
          written in memory of Lalo's wife, Noémi.

Line 16   Although Bérenice is the goddess of victory, Proust
          is also most likely referring to the character in the
          play of that name by Jean Racine, one of his favor-
          ite writers. In the play, the emperor Titus is forced
          by circumstances to give up the woman he loves
          and send her away. Like Lucienne Bréval, Bérénice
          is foreign-born.

          Note: Proust wrote to Hahn that the poem was
          unfinished "owing to an attack" (*une crise*).

POEM 50
Translated by Mark Polizzotti

Written in early August 1906 (most likely at the Hôtel des Rés-
ervoirs in Versailles) and sent to Reynaldo Hahn.

Line 4   The florist Maison Debac was located at 63, bou-
          levard Malesherbes. See also Poem 70 and notes.

Line 6   Camille Saint-Saëns (1835–1921) was a composer,
          conductor, and organist. One of his pupils was
          Gabriel Fauré. It is often thought that the work of
          Saint-Saëns was used as one of the models for Vin-
          teuil's sonata in RTP.

Though Proust was friends with the writer Comte Alexandre de Gabriac (he wrote a pastiche of his work in 1908), this most likely refers to Comte Arthur de Gabriac, the French baritone and interpreter of the work of Fauré.

Line 8   Daniel de Losques (né Henri Daniel Casimir Paul Thouroude, 1880–1915) was an illustrator for several publications, including *Le Figaro*, and a poster artist. He was killed in World War I.

Sigismund-Ferdinand Bach, known as Bac (1859–1952) was a painter and illustrator. He was a close friend of Proust's as well as of Marie-Thérèse de Chevigné's, daughter of Comte and Comtesse Adhéaume de Chevigné.

Lines 12   Because this poem refers to an aria, Proust may be
and 14   confusing the names in the biblical story of Rebecca and Eleazar (Genesis 24) and those in Fromental Halévy's *La Juive* (see notes to Poem 3), in which the main character's name is Rachel.

Line 18   Adèle-Victorine Isaac (1854–1915) was a singer in the Opéra-Comique.

Geraldine Farrar (1882–1967) was an American singer. She was scheduled to sing the role of Zerlina in *Don Giovanni* in Salzburg, where Hahn would be conducting. After a career in Europe, Farrar returned to the United States and became a star at the Metropolitan Opera, as well as in silent films; she played the lead role in the movie of Georges Bizet's *Carmen*.

Line 20   Reference to Mozart's *Le nozze di Figaro, ossia,
           La folle giornata* (*The Marriage of Figaro, or, The
           Day of Madness*), with a libretto based on a play
           by Beaumarchais and the scene with Countess
           Rosina Almaviva and the page Cherubino.

Line 23   Comte Robert d'Aramon, a friend of Proust, was
           far enough inside Proust's circle to often be called
           Nomara.

Line 24   François-Marie-Pons-Louis, Marquis de Dadisart,
           was born in 1875.

Line 26   Vincent Griffon was the head clinician at the
           Hôtel-Dieu (main hospital). He had interned with
           Proust's brother, Robert.

Line 27   Jean-Nicolas Corvisart (1755–1821) was, from
           1804 to 1815, primary physician to Napoleon I.

Line 28   Lilli Lehmann (1848–1929) was an operatic so-
           prano and, later, founder of the International
           Summer Academy at the Mozarteum in Salzburg.
           She would share responsibility with Hahn for the
           Vienna Philharmonic Orchestra at Salzburg that
           summer.

Line 38   The Russian singer Félia Litvinne (née Françoise
           Jeanne Schutz, 1860–1936) was considered one of
           the foremost dramatic sopranos of her day, spe-
           cializing in Wagnerian roles and performing both
           in Europe and America. Her sister, Hélène, was
           married to the great operatic bass Edouard de
           Reszke. Some critics said that her vocal talents
           could not compare with Lilli Lehmann.

POEM 51

Translated by Nicholas Christopher with Ana Oancea

Line 2   Jean Cocteau (1889–1963). For more information on Proust and Cocteau, see Poem 96.

Line 3   Lucien most likely refers to Lucien Daudet (1878–1946), son of novelist Alphonse Daudet, younger brother of Léon Daudet, a writer and a friend of both Proust and Cocteau (he had introduced the two of them). Proust reviewed Lucien Daudet's collection of four novellas, *Le Prince des Cravates*, which he had dedicated to Proust, in the *Intransigeant* on October 21, 1910. For his previous review, of Lucien's *Le Chemin Mort*, he had used the pseudonym Marc Eodonte, a play on Marcel Dante.

Line 5   May refer to Edouard Hermann. See Poem 43 and its notes.

Line 6   Vaslav Nijinsky (1890–1950) was the foremost dancer of his day, appearing with Sergei Diaghilev's Ballets Russes in Paris and creating sensations in, among other performances, *Petrouchka*, *The Afternoon of a Faun*, and *The Rite of Spring*, the last of which caused near riots. It was produced at the new Théâtre des Champs-Elysées by Proust's close friend Gabriel Astruc.

Line 8   Léon Bakst (né Lev Samoylovich Rosenberg, 1866–1924) was a painter and illustrator who designed many of the sets for Diaghilev's Ballets Russes.

Line 10   Paul Ernest Boniface de Castellane (1867–1932), a
           celebrated Paris dandy, married American Anna
           Gould, daughter of Jay Gould, as his own fortune
           dwindled. When he began to dissipate her for-
           tune as well, she divorced him and married his
           cousin Hélie de Talleyrand-Périgord, duc de Sa-
           gan. Boni de Castellane (as he was generally
           known) later traveled in America and produced
           two entertaining memoirs, *Comment j'ai decou-
           vert l'Amérique* (*How I Discovered America*) and
           L'Art d'être pauvre: Memoires (The Art of Being
           Poor: Memoirs).

POEM 52

Translated by Rosanna Warren

Line 1   Bertrand Sauvan d'Aramon (1876–1949) was a
           politician.

Line 30   Marie-Amédée-Henri-Napoleón Gourgaud (1881–
           1944) was a friend of Proust, nicknamed Napo.
           Proust wrote to Hahn that he would be doing a
           pastiche of him. Gourgaud became an important
           collector of impressionist and modern art as well
           as artifacts he acquired on trips to Africa. Count
           Antoine Sala was a diplomat whose flamboyantly
           gay behavior led Proust to create the noun "Sala-
           ïsm." Proust mentions him in the *Carnet* of 1908,
           with regard to "old age."

POEM 53
Translated by Rosanna Warren

Line 3   Editor's note: I will speculate that this refers to Fer-
           dinand of Bulgaria (1861–1948), who was married
           but who, it was rumored, had many homosexual
           affairs. At the age of forty-seven, for political rea-
           sons he married Eleonore Caroline Gasparine Lou-
           ise, Princess Reuss-Köstritz, who may be the
           "Princess Elchie" referred to in line 28. The "Rus-
           sian" in line 1 may refer to the dominance of Bul-
           garia by Russia.

Line 10   Dinant is a city on the River Meuse known for its
           metallurgy.

Line 21   For Antoine Sala, see note to line 30 in Poem 52
           above.

Line 26   *Le Fils de Coralie* (The Sons of Coralie) is a novel
           by Albert Delpit (1849–1893).

POEM 54
Translated by Jennifer Moxley

Lines 6   St. Medardus is the patron saint of shelter from
and 7   bad weather.

Lines 11   Note that in the French original note Proust used
and 16   the phrase "jeunes filles en fleurs," which he also
           used for the title of the second volume of RTP (*À
           l'ombre des jeunes filles en fleurs*).

Poems 55 to 98: Poèmes à / Poems to . . .

Although poems that Francis and Gontier placed earlier in their collection were dedicated to specific individuals, the editors of that French journal issue judiciously placed Proust's adult poems in the separate category of "Poèmes à" (Poems to). Though Proust dedicated poems to many of his friends, as with his letters, the largest number were meant for Reynaldo Hahn, and often only for him. Hahn represented a unique relationship in Proust's life. He was born in Caracas, Venezuela, in either 1874 or 1875 (depending on the source). His family moved to France in 1879, where Hahn became known as a musical prodigy and was invited to important salons. In May 1894, Proust and Hahn met at the Paris home of painter Madeleine Lemaire, and took to one another immediately; they then spent time at her house in the country, the Château de Réveillon. They collaborated on a song cycle of Proust's "Portraits de peintres" and then "Portraits de musiciens," and contemplated a joint biography of Chopin. Their relationship probably began as a sexual affair, but seems to have evolved into "une amitié amoureuse."

Proust and Hahn exchanged at least 186 letters (the most recent count by Martin Robitaille) and, according to Céleste Albaret, Hahn was the only person who could enter Proust's room unannounced. Hahn was a highly acclaimed musician and composer in his time, but today is known mostly for his art songs. Proust and Hahn's letters are speckled with a childlike (and childish) use of reconstituted spellings, with the addition of an "s" before soft consonants, at least twelve pet names such as Bunibuls, Guncht, and Buncht, and "wicked" satires on people they knew (several times Proust asked Hahn to burn a letter after reading it). Hahn was also close to the actress Sarah Bernhardt and the cocotte Méry Laurent, who was the lover of Edouard Manet; Napoleon III's wealthy American-born dentist, Thomas Evans; and Stéphane Mallarmé. At her death, she left Hahn her home and all its contents. Hahn died in 1947.

POEM 55

Translated by Wayne Koestenbaum

Reynaldo Hahn had a long-haired basset hound. See Poem 57 and its note for more information.

POEM 56

Translated by Harold Augenbraum

POEM 57

Translated by Nicholas Christopher with Ana Oancea

Zadig was the main character in Voltaire's 1743 *Zadig ou la destinée* (*Zadig, or, The Book of Fate*) but it was also the name of Reynaldo Hahn's dog, a long-haired basset hound. In Yiddish, a *zadig* is a righteous man.

POEM 58

Translated by Marcella Durand and Michel Durand

Sent to Hahn, accompanied by a line drawing of a scene consisting of four people as if seen through a double, peaked doorway divided by a narrow column. Most likely composed in 1904.

Line 3   Félicie Fitau and Marie (last name unknown) were maids for Proust's family when they lived at 45, rue de Courcelles. The former would remain in his service until July 1, 1907. She was one of the models for Françoise in *Contre Saint-Beuve* and RTP.

Line 5   In order to assuage his asthma, Proust regularly
burned Legras powder in his room, but the smoke
often disturbed his neighbors. See Paul Morand's
poem "To Marcel Proust" in the notes to Poem
102. Céleste Albaret's *Monsieur Proust* is a good
source of information on how Proust used this
powder (as well Espic's anti-asthma cigarettes).

POEM 59
Translated by Marcella Durand and Michel Durand

POEM 60
Translated by Cole Swensen

POEM 61
Translated by Jennifer Moxley

POEM 62
Translated by Nicholas Christopher with Ana Oancea

Albert Sorel (1842–1906) was Proust's professor of history in the
École libre d'études politiques de Paris (Sciences-Po) as well as a
poet and composer. Proust sent him this pastiche in verse in
April 1905.

POEM 63

Translated by Rosanna Warren

According to Kolb, this poem was written in July 1906.

Line 5   The stock market quotations appeared on the next
to last page of the newspaper *Le Figaro*.

Line 12   Lady Robert de Rothschild, née Anspach. See
notes to Poem 47 for more information. Also see
line 26 of this poem.

Line 14   Angelo Poliziano (1454–1494), the author of
the poem "Orpheus."

Line 20   Hahn would be going to Salzburg to conduct Mo-
zart's *Don Giovanni*. See notes to Poem 68.

Line 25   The Rothschild banking offices were located at
21, rue Laffite.

Line 29   Henri Cain (1857–1937) was a dramatist and col-
lector of art of the eighteenth century best known
today for the libretti he wrote for opera and ballet,
including several for Jules Massenet. He was mar-
ried to the lyric soprano Julia Guiraudon, who in
1898 performed Mimi in *La Bohème* in its first
French performance. In 1899 she created the role
of Cinderella in Massenet's *Cendrillon*, with a li-
bretto by her future husband.

Line 30   Founder of the anti-Semitic newspaper *La Libre Parole*, Edouard-Adolphe Drumont (1844–1917) was the best-known anti-Semite in France. He also founded the political group Action Française and authored the book *La France Juive* (Jewish France, 1886), which sold over 100,000 copies.

Line 31   Lecoffre was a well-known bookshop and publisher.

Line 33   In 1905, the French government passed the law of separation of church and state.

Line 38   Raymond Poincaré (1860–1934) was the minister of finance at the time this poem was written.

Line 44   The Marquise Louis Suchet d'Albufera, née Anna-Victoire-Andrée Masséna de Rivoli.

Line 49   In 1905, the Russians and Japanese engaged in a brief war that was disastrous for both the Russian polity and its economy.

Line 52   On April 17, 1906, Tsar Nicholas II issued a ukase (imperial decree) announcing that his government would be issuing bonds payable at 5 percent. They had previously paid 3 percent.

POEM 64

Translated by Wyatt Mason

Embedded in a letter to Reynaldo Hahn written in mid-August 1906.

The poem was inspired by Proust looking out his window in the Hôtel des Réservoirs in Versailles and catching a glimpse of a valet who looked familiar from another time and place in his life. Kolb finds an echo of Pascal in their exchange.

POEM 65

Translated by Jennifer Moxley

Written just before September 19, 1906, and sent from the Hôtel des Réservoirs in Versailles.

Line 4   Allusion to *Clara d'Ellébeuse, or, The Story of an Old Young Girl* by Francis Jammes. Kolb speculates that Pelénor is a conflation of the names Pelléas and Aliénor. Jammes was a personal favorite of Proust whom he once called one of the best writers of the time.

Line 5   Léon was a manservant at the Hôtel des Réservoirs.

Line 6   In Greek mythology, Orpheus wanders endlessly looking for an audience for his music.

Line 11   Auguste was a manservant in Hahn's household.

Line 16   The Greek-born symbolist poet Yánnis Papadiamantópoulos (1856–1910) wrote French poetry and prose under the name of Jean Moréas. He issued several poetry manifestoes; Proust did not think very highly of his work. See Proust's brief essay "La jeunesse flagornée" ("The Fawning of Young Poets") in *Essais et articles*.

Line 19   Most likely refers to Mario de La Tour Saint-Ygest, a poet and disciple of Leconte de Lisle who published poetry in *La Grande Revue*. He was married to Claudine, daughter of Catulle-Mendès and Augusta Holmes. A portrait of her and her sisters by Pierre-Auguste Renoir is in the collection of the Metropolitan Museum of Art.

Line 20   Fernand Gregh (1873–1960) was a poet and literary critic. He and Proust met at the Lycée Condorcet and collaborated on several small literary magazines, including *Le Banquet*.

           Most likely the playwright René Peter (1842–1947). He and Proust were brought together as children by their fathers' shared profession and then became friends again after the success of Peter's play *Chiffon* in 1904.

Line 22   Fernand Labori (1860–1917) was Émile Zola's defense attorney in the trial over the "J'accuse" article in the Dreyfus affair, and later Colonel Picquart's (and represented Dreyfus). Proust would write him an admiring letter when he survived an assassination attempt in 1899, in which, on his way to defend Dreyfus, he was shot. Eight days later he appeared in court on Dreyfus's behalf.

           According to Kolb, Joseph Hild was an attorney who worked with Labori.

Line 23   Jean de Castellane (1868–1965) was the brother of Proust's close friend Boni de Castellane.

Line 24 Robert de Rothschild (1880–1946) was the son of
Baron Gustave de Rothschild.

Line 28 For information on Marie Nordlinger, see notes to
Poem 82.

POEM 66

Translated by Harold Augenbraum

According to Kolb's dating, this poem was sent to Reynaldo
Hahn in a letter on November 16, 1906. In Kolb's edition of
Proust's letters to Hahn (1956), it ends after line 5 but in the col-
lected letters line 6 is included. Francis and Gontier note that it
is a pastiche of Corneille's *Le Cid*. It most likely refers to a pas-
sage in act I, scene iii:

 « Enfin vous l'emporter, et le faveur du roi
 Vous élève en un rang qui n'était dû qu'à moi »

Line 1 Paul Reboux (né André Amilet, 1877–1963) was
best known for his humorous pastiches of contem-
porary writers, which were collected in the books
À la manière de . . . (In the Style of . . .), written
with Charles Muller. He was also a literary and
food critic and codirector (with Proust's Lycée
Condorcet friend Fernand Gregh) of the journal
Les Lettres. Kolb suggests that Proust is referring
here to Hahn's having written music for Reboux's
poem "Prometheus Triumphant."

Line 3 Proust met Henri Bardac (ca. 1885–1951) in 1906
through Hahn. In a letter, Proust described Bar-
dac as "a guinea pig in pink coral." Bardac would
introduce Proust to Paul Morand (see Poem 102
and its note).

Fernand Ochsé (1879–1945) was an artist, composer, and friend of both Proust and Hahn (as was his brother Julien). He was deported during the Occupation and died in Auschwitz.

Walter Marrast (1876–1933) was known professionally as Walther Straram (an anagram of his last name, which his musician father had used before him; he added the "h" to his first name in homage to the character in Wagner's *Die Meistersinger*). He was born in London and conducted at the Paris Opera and the Opéra-Comique. When this letter was written, he had just been named choral director at the opera.

Line 5   Though Proust had many friends of this name, this Léon most likely refers to the manservant at the Hôtel des Réservoirs, where Proust was living while 102, boulevard Haussmann was undergoing renovation.

Line 6   Soon after they met, Hahn gave Proust the pet names of *poney* and *poulain* (both translate in English as "pony"). Their correspondence was often playful. In a letter from Proust to Hahn, sent from Trouville and which Philip Kolb has dated September 16, 1894, Proust opens with the words "Mon petit maître" (in English, "My little master") and later asks Hahn, "Why 'Marcel le poney?'" Yet, he closes the letter with "Votre poney, Marcel." See also poems 71, 72, and 76.

POEM 67

Translated by Anna Moschovakis

Sent as part of the same letter as Poem 65 above.

Line 3   *La Vierge d'Avila* (The Virgin of Avila) was a play
            by Catulle-Mendès (1841–1909) which was pre-
            miered on November 10, 1906, with Sarah Bern-
            hardt in the role of Saint Teresa.

POEM 68

Translated by Susan Stewart

Sent to Reynaldo Hahn in the early part of December 1906
from the Hôtel des Réservoirs in Versailles, where Proust was
living while his aunt's apartment at 102, boulevard Haussmann
was being renovated for his use (for more information, see notes
to Poem 49). Proust suggested that Hahn not leave this letter ly-
ing around because of the references to Chevigné and Pourtalès.

Line 3   Based on the great success of his *Don Giovanni*
            in Salzburg that year, one Mr. Aronson invited
            Hahn for an American tour and Hahn was sched-
            uled to leave on Christmas Eve. Mr. Aronson can-
            celed the tour, claiming that concerts were not
            doing well that year, and it was put off to the fol-
            lowing. Hahn admitted that he hadn't wanted to
            go and he "allowed it to disappear," according to
            Hahn biographer Bernard Gavoty.

Line 6   With Porte-Batôn, Proust may be referring to him-
            self, since he often described himself as "the her-
            mit of Versailles."

Line 7   In 1895, Reynaldo Hahn lived in the home of Ma-
              dame Charles Dettelbach, 13, rue Christophe Co-
              lomb. She was a member of the Sociéte des amis
              de la musique (Society of Friends of Music) and an
              intimate of Gabriel Fauré, who dedicated several
              pieces of music to her.

              Count Adhéaume de Chevigné, who died in 1911.
              For related information, see notes to Poem 6.

Line 13   Grand Duke Vladimir-Alexandrovitch Romanov
              (1847–1909), a member of the Russian royal fam-
              ily, was a fixture in Parisian society. Proust and
              his friends often made fun of his strong accent.

Line 17   Proust was good friends with the Foulds: father,
              banker Léon (1839–1924), son Eugène, and daugh-
              ter Élisabeth.

Line 18   Most likely a reference to the American family of
              Anna Gould, wife of Proust's great friend Boni de
              Castellane, daughter of Jay Gould.

Line 19   Countess Edmond de Pourtalès, (née Mélanie de
              Bussière). She was celebrated for her elegance.

Line 23   Proust added his own note to Hahn: "Consul
              General of France in New York."

Line 26   Reskés de Noufflard refers to the brothers Ed-
              ouard and Jean de Reszké, bass and tenor at the
              Paris Opera. Maurice Noufflard (1874–1933) was
              a student of the latter. His brother Charles (1972–
              1951) was the colonial governor of Gabon at the
              time.

POEM 69

Translated by Wayne Koestenbaum

Sent to Reynaldo Hahn in a letter in early December 1906. In a letter dated "Versailles, mardi soir 11 décembre 1906," Proust discusses the purchase of shares in the Compagnie de tramways electric, explaining the idea of a "gift."

POEM 70

Translated by Wyatt Mason

Written in early December, 1906, at the Hôtel des Réservoirs in Versailles, Tadié notes that this poem is a parody of Kleinzach's ballad in the prologue to Offenbach's *Tales of Hoffmann*. In this poem, Proust may have sacrificed meaning to rhyme.

Line 2   The florist Maison Debac was located at 63, boulevard Malesherbes (Debac also appears in Poem 50).

Line 3   Philip Kolb suggests that "Esbac" refers to Achille Essebac (né Bécasse, 1868–1936), the author of the novels *Dédé*, a homoerotic novel, and *Les Griffes*. On the verso of the paper on which this poem was written are the words "je lis Esbac" (I read Esbac).

Line 4   Schwabach is a town in Germany known for the creation of a typeface called Schwabacher.

Line 5   Washington, DC, lies on the Potomac River. Kolb speculates that Hahn may have been planning a trip to the United States (see Poem 68 and its notes).

Line 7   This most likely refers to Sulzbach, a town in Germany, but in a letter to Hahn written in 1895, Proust notes that he had spoken at length that evening with a Madame Sulzbach, who said that "she would give all of Beethoven for one piece by Fauré."

Line 8   Proust had proposed to Hahn that they travel together to Brittany.

Line 9   For information on Gustava Anspach, see notes to Poem 47.

Line 11   Henri Bardac studied at Oxford University. For information on Bardac, see notes to Poem 66.

Line 12   Proust so greatly admired Prince Edmond de Polignac, who was a composer and, in particular, a great music patron that he asked his widow if he could dedicate the second volume of RTP, *À l'ombre jes jeunes filles en fleurs*, to him. His widow asked that he not do so.

Line 21   This refers to Count Robert de Montesquiou-Fézensac. For more information, see the notes to Poem 44.

Line 22   Philip Alexius de László (1869–1937) was a Hungarian painter famous for his society portraits, among them the Duke and Duchess de Gramont.

            Franz von Lenbach (1836–1904) was a German painter of the realist school known for his portraits of the powerful, including Otto von Bismark and Lady Curzon.

POEM 71

Translated by Harold Augenbraum

Sent to Reynaldo Hahn, probably from the Hôtel des Réservoirs in Versailles, in December 1906.

Line 1   Louis Legendre (1851–1908) was a poet and dramatist. Among his books are *Le Bruit et le silence* (Noise and Silence) and *Musiques d'automnes* (Autumn Music).

Line 2   Hugues Delorme (né Georges Thiébost, 1868–1942), known as La Voltige because of his towering height, was a humorist and writer of comic operettas and cabaret songs, as well as appreciations of the caricaturists SEM and Carlègle.

Line 3   Jean-Louis Vaudoyer (1883–1963) was a novelist and art historian and administrator general of the Comédie-Française from 1941 to 1944, during the Occupation. He was Daniel Halévy's brother-in-law and published Halévy's *Pays Parisiens* in his series Portraits de la France. He was also a close friend of Proust, particularly during the last decade of Proust's life when they often went to look at art together. In May 1921, spurred by Vaudoyer's article, Proust asked Vaudoyer to accompany him to the Musée Jeu de Paume to see an exhibition on Dutch art, which included Vermeer's *View of Delft*.

Line 5   Léo Larguier (1878–1950) was a poet, critic, and essayist.

Line 8   Lionel des Rieux (1870–1915) was a poet and literary critic.

POEM 72
Translated by Jennifer Moxley

Line 1   For information on Paul Ernest Boniface de Castellane (1867–1932), see note to Poem 51.

Lines 3   The conservative writer and politician Maurice
and 4   Barrès (1862–1923) was born in Charmes, which
            sits on the River Moselle about two hundred miles
            east of Paris.

Line 8   Rosalie von Gutmann (the Comtesse de Fitz-James, 1862–1923) was so unhappily married to the Comte that wags called her Rosa Malheur (Rosa Unhappiness), a play on the name of the painter Rosa Bonheur. For more information, see notes to Poem 43.

Line 12   Hopilliart et Leroy were furniture makers and antiques dealers in the rue des Saint Pères. In April 1910, Proust purchased engravings there.

            Risler et Carré were silversmiths in the rue du Faubourg Saint-Honoré.

Line 14   "Venise," also known as "Venise la rouge" or "Dans la Venise la Rouge," which are derived from its first line, is a poem by Alfred de Musset, published in 1828. Charles Gounod set it to music in 1849.

Line 18   The references to the Institut (de France) and
            (Jeanne) Raunay most likely are the result of
            Proust's teasing Hahn about professional jealousy.
            Over a period of about five years (1906–10), Ga-
            briel Fauré composed the song cycle "La Chanson
            d'ève," which was premiered by the mezzo so-
            prano Jeanne Raunay. In 1909, Fauré, who was
            known to be ambitious, was elected to member-
            ship in the prestigious Institut. In 1911, he pub-
            lished the cycle, dedicated to Raunay.

Line 20   For more information on the term of endearment
            "pony," see notes to Poem 66.

                        POEM 73
                Translated by Harold Augenbraum

Line 1   Perhaps Alexis Jacques Marie Wafflard (1787–
            1824), a dramatist born in Versailles? His most
            famous works were *A Moment of Imprudence*
            (1819) and *Voyage to Dieppe* (1821).

            According to Francis and Gontier, Brack refers to
            Alexandre Bracke (1861–1955) a Hellenist and
            politician.

            Collardeau may refer to Charles-Pierre Colardeau
            (1732–1776), a playwright.

Line 9   Jeanne-Louise Dejarny-Brindeau, whose stage name was Jeanne Brindeau (1860–1946), was an actress with the Comédie-Française and later in films. Anatole France's dalliance with her almost drove Mme Arman de Caillavet to suicide. Hahn's close friend Méry Laurent left her a pair of diamond earrings in her will.

Line 13   Marie-Thérèse Kolb (1856–?) was a member of the acting troupe of the Comédie-Française.

Tosca, an opera by Giacomo Puccini.

Hahn wrote the four-act musical comedy *La Carmélite* in 1902, with book by Catulle-Mendès. It was produced at the Opéra-Comique in December of that year.

Line 15   The Marquis de Modène is mentioned in RTP with the Baron de Charlus. He is also mentioned in Edmund de Waal's *The Hare with Amber Eyes* as having attended a party at the Ephrussi home.

The Camandos, a family of wealthy Jews with whom Proust was friendly, particularly with Moise (born 1860) and Nissim. Their remaining members were deported in the 1940s and died in a Nazi concentration camp.

d'Albu refers to Louis, Marquis d'Albufera, close friend of Proust for whom the latter acted as a go-between between him and his mistress, Louisa de Mornand (see Poem 93 and its notes).

Line 20   Opened in 1858, the El Dorado was a large *café concert* located at 4, boulevard Strasbourg. In *Souvenir Portraits*, Jean Cocteau writes that he and his friends would take a box and then wait outside at the rear entrance on the Faubourg Saint-Martin afterward for the performers to emerge.

Line 21   Born in London, Harry Fragson (né Léon Philippe Pot, 1869–1913), a well-known music hall singer of the time in both London and Paris, was a friend of Proust's and Hahn's. He also sang at the Folies-Bergères and in private salons. According to contemporary accounts, Fragson died when his father, believing that Harry was about to put him in a retirement home, shot him as he entered the apartment they shared on the rue Lafayette.

Line 22   Maurice de Féraudy (1859–1932) was a French actor best known for his performance in the comedy *Les Affaires sont les affaires* (Business is Business), which he performed over twelve hundred times.

Leonard Sylvain Julien (Jules) Sandeau (1811–1883) was a French novelist and playwright who is best remembered today as the early collaborator of Madame Dudevant's, who later adapted their joint pseudonym, J. Sand, into her pen name, George Sand. He also collaborated with Émile Augier on various plays (see notes to Poem 74 for more information on Augier). Sandeau was also one of the writers who collaborated on Théophile Gautier's epistolary novel *La Croix de Berny* (*The Cross of Berny*), which Proust and his friends from *Le Banquet* used as a model for an abortive novel of the same type.

Line 28   *La Sulamite* was a song cycle by composer Emmanuel Chabrier (1841–1894) with lyrics by Jean Richepin, adapted from the biblical Song of Songs.

POEM 74
Translated by Marcella Durand and Michel Durand

In 1894, the French military command came to believe that there was a leak in its intelligence division and that someone was passing military secrets to the German army. In order to ensure the integrity of its work, and needing someone to blame, it accused Captain Alfred Dreyfus, a Jewish officer, of the crime, which he denied. Despite flimsy evidence, which turned out later to have been falsified, Dreyfus was sentenced to exile on Devil's Island.

When the falsification of the *bordereau* (memorandum) came to light, France divided into two camps: Dreyfusard and anti-Dreyfusard. It is hard to describe the vehemence of the split. Longtime friendships ended and one's identity and social life were often dictated by where one's sentiments lay. At some point, even Dreyfus's guilt or innocence became secondary to the honor of the French army and the importance of maintaining a united front in the face of the German threat. The Dreyfus Affair, as it came to be known, plays an important role in RTP. Proust was good friends with Joseph Reinach (1856–921), who wrote a six-volume *Histoire de l'affaire Dreyfus*, though they later fell out.

Although Francis and Gontier put them together, these stanzas seem to have been written at different times. The first was included in a letter to Reynaldo Hahn around December 15, 1906.

Line 1   Marie-Georges Picquart (1854–1914), a lieutenant
          colonel in the French army, was a central figure in
          the Dreyfus case. He discovered and reported
          what he believed was a forgery of the papers that
          incriminated Dreyfus and subsequently was trans-
          ferred to duty in southern Tunisia. After it became
          clear that he was indeed correct and Dreyfus was
          exonerated, Picquart was restored to the army,
          later becoming a general and minister of war.
          Proust was introduced to Picquart by their mutual
          friend Louis de Robert, and admired him, but be-
          came disillusioned later when Picquart was the
          minister of war.

          Aline Ménard-Dorian (1850–1929) held a republi-
          can salon that was a hotbed of Dreyfusism. Léon
          Daudet once mocked her as "Picquart's fortress."

Line 2   Proust visited with the Comte and Comtesse
          d'Arnoux when he was staying in Versailles in the
          fall of 1906. In a postscript to a letter to Reynaldo
          Hahn, he described the comte as trying to imitate
          the reserve of Jacques Hébrard, former senator of
          French India.

Line 3   Alvarez (né Albert Gourron, 1861–1933) was a
          star of the Paris Opera.

Line 6   Kolb speculates that this refers to either Max
          Leclerc, an editor at the *Journal de débats*, or Paul
          Leclercq, a writer and critic who was a childhood
          friend of Proust. It could also be Henri Leclerc, an
          anthologist, or one of a few others of the same
          name in Proust's life.

Line 7   Henri-Gabriel Ibels (1867–1936) was a French
          painter and graphic artist, and member of the ar-
          tistic group Les Nabis.

Line 9   This may be an allusion to Émile Augier's 1878
          play *Les Fourchambault*, in which a passing refer-
          ence to Odysseus's wife is lost on a handsome but
          dim-witted young man.

POEM 75
Translated by Marcella Durand and Michel Durand

Francis and Gontier note that this is a pastiche of Alfred de
Musset's poem "La Nuit d'Octobre":

C'était, il m'en souvient par une nuit d'automne
Triste et froide, à peu près semblable à celle-ci
Le murmure du vent de son bruit monotone
Dans mon cerveau lassé berçait mon noir souci
J'étais à la fenêtre, attendant ma maîtresse.

'Twas an autumnal evening, I recall,
Chill, gloomy; this one brings it back again.
The murmuring wind's monotonous rise and fall
Lulled sombre care within my weary brain.
I waited at the casement for my love . . .

Translated by Emma Lazarus

POEM 76
Translated by Marcella Durand and Michel Durand

POEM 77

Translated by Mary Ann Caws

Written in July 1911.

POEM 78

Translated by Wayne Koestenbaum

A longer version of this poem was discovered in Proust's exercise book of 1890. Proust met Robert de Billy (1869–1953) during his military service in Orleans and then both studied at the École libre des sciences politiques. He entered the French foreign service and was often dispatched to embassies around the world.

POEM 79

Translated by Wayne Koestenbaum

Written about Robert de Billy (see note to Poem 78), who was very reserved.

POEM 80

Translated by Mark Polizzotti

Madeleine Lemaire (1845–1928) was considered the greatest painter of flowers of a generation in which flowers were a significant theme. Her lover, Alexandre Dumas *fils*, once said, "After God, she created the most roses."

Lemaire lived at 31, rue du Monceau with her daughter Suzette. There every Tuesday they held a salon—they were often lumped together as "Les Veuves"—The Widows—attracting such stalwarts of the demimonde and artistic world as the playwright Victorien Sardou, the poet Comte Robert de Montesquiou, the composer Saint-Saëns, the actor/director Charles Le Bargy, and the singer Jean de Reszké. On May 22, 1894, in Lemaire's salon, Proust met the nineteen-year-old Hahn at one of

Lemaire's musical evenings where the entertainment was poems from Montesquiou's collection *Les Chauves-souris* (The Bats) set to music by Léon Delafosse (see notes to Poem 32). One of the first performances of Proust and Hahn's "Portraits de peintres" took place at her home on May 28, 1895, with Édouard Risler at the piano. She illustrated the first edition of Proust's *Les Plaisirs et les jours* (which was originally titled "Le Château de Réveillon"), including the drawing for the short story "Le Diner en ville" ("Dinner in the City"), using the likenesses of Proust and Suzette. SEM created a lively caricature of Hahn, Lemaire, and Montesquiou, which is currently in the collection of the Bibliothèque Nationale de France. Lemaire is often thought to be one of the models for Mme Verdurin in RTP.

POEM 81

Translated by Mary Ann Caws

See Poem 80 and its notes for information on Madeleine Lemaire and her painting.

POEM 82

Translated by Susan Stewart

Marie Nordlinger (1876–1961) was the English-born cousin of Reynaldo Hahn and a talented craft sculptress. She and Proust became very close, particularly after she took over from his mother the duties of helping him with his translations of works by John Ruskin. She is said to have given him the pressed Japanese flowers which, when put into water, unfold into animal shapes, providing the basis for a key image in the madeleine scene in RTP. For an appreciation of the relationship among the three, see P. F. Prestwich, *The Translation of Memories*. As is his wont, Proust peppers the poem with references to the subject's works, in this case, Ruskin's *Sesame and Lilies*, *The Stones of Venice*, and *The Bible of Amiens*.

POEM 83
Translated by Jeff Clark

Sent in a letter to Louisa de Mornand. Mornand (née Louise Montaud, 1884–1963) was an actress whose lover was Proust's great friend the Marquis d'Albufera. There has been speculation that she and Proust had a sexual liaison; the biographer George D. Painter flatly states that they did, based chiefly on an interview Mornand gave to the newsweekly *Candide* on the occasion of the 1928 publication of her letters from Proust. Antonio de La Gandara painted her portrait seated with a small dog in her lap, which is now in the collection of the Musée des Beaux Arts in Grenoble (depending on the source, dated either 1903 or 1907).

After a career on the stage, Mornand appeared in a dozen films, generally playing an older aristocrat. For more information on Mornand, see Poem 93 and its note. In Mina Curtiss's *Other People's Letters*, Curtiss went to visit Proust's former housekeeper, Céleste, who told her that Louisa de Mornand once came to see her and that she looked like "une grosse concierge" (a big fat doorkeep).

POEM 84
Translated by Mary Ann Caws

Proust met Prince Antoine Bibesco (1878–1951) and his brother Emmanuel in 1899. An admired diplomat, Bibesco later became a successful playwright. He soon formed part of Proust's inner circle.

Although Bibesco was married to Elizabeth Asquith— daughter of British prime minister Herbert Henry Asquith, sister of film director Anthony Asquith, and half sister to Violet Bonham-Carter—he was known for his many love affairs, particularly after his wife's death. In her 1978 book *Other People's Letters*, the writer Mina Curtiss tells the charming story of going to Paris in 1948 as a woman in her twenties to search for

Proust's letters. Bibesco had published a book of Proust's letters to him, but they were truncated, and Curtiss wanted to see the originals. She met Bibesco, then close to seventy and still living in his lovely apartment on the île St. Louis, and was instantly charmed, but before he was willing to show her the letters he required her to make love with him. Not only did she agree, and enjoyed her time with him, but later when she met another of Bibesco's recent "conquests" they swapped stories and had a pleasant and affectionate conversation about him.

POEM 85
Translated by Mary Ann Caws

POEM 86
Translated by Marcella Durand and Michel Durand

According to Kolb, this seems to have been written in March or April 1902.

Line 1   "La Lutte" was a play by Antoine Bibesco, produced in 1902.

Line 8   Georges de Porto-Riche (1849–1930) was a French playwright who frequented some of the same salons as Proust, despite, as William Carter has noted, an avowed dislike of the aristocracy.

Line 12   Philip Kolb does not gloss Colette and suggests
            that Suzanne is the actress Suzanne Devoyod
            (1866–1954) who would later play a role in Bibes-
            co's 1904 play *Le Jaloux* (though instead Suzanne
            may refer to Louisa de Mornand's sister, Suzanne
            Montaud, since in the entry in his *Carnet of 1908*
            (Notebook of 1908), Proust suggests that Suzanne
            was Fénelon's lover). Florence Callu and Antoine
            Compagnon, the editors of the *carnets*, add that
            Suzanne, like her sister, was an actress who used
            the name Jeanne Moriane. According to William
            Carter's biography, she acted in "the Bouffes"
            (Théâtre des Bouffes-Parisien) under the name of
            Jane Moriane. For more information on Louisa
            de Mornand, see notes to Poem 83. Additional
            note: not only was Proust friendly at the time with
            the writer and performer Colette, who also lived
            on rue de Courcelles, he was also close to Hélène
            de Caraman-Chimay (Bibesco was her cousin)
            and the poem may refer to them.

            Antoine Bibesco's aunt (née Marie Bibesco) was
            the Comtesse Odon de Montesquiou-Fézensac
            and hence Antoine and his brother Emmanuel
            were Robert de Montesquiou's cousins. In her
            memoir *Au Bal avec Marcel Proust*, Marthe
            Bibesco tells of meeting Montesquiou, who, when
            he was told her name, said, "I hope you are not
            related to those two awful Bibesco brothers." She
            responded that yes, they were her cousins.

POEM 87
Translated by Marcella Durand and Michel Durand

Line 6   *Jacques Abran* [sic] was a three-act play by Antoine Bibesco, produced at the Théâtre Rejane in 1910.

Line 12   Émile Picot (1844–1918) was a linguist and bibliographer. He was known for his study of medieval and Renaissance literature. Proust wrote to him in January 1904 requesting information on the etymology of the name of the German town of Eisenbach for his translation of *The Bible of Amiens*.

Line 13   Michel Bréal (1832–1915) was a linguist. His son Auguste (1867–1941) was a painter and art historian.

            Louis Petit de Julleville (1841–1900) was a historian of French theater.

Line 14   Sabran refers either to St. Elzear of Sabran or Louis de Sabran, a French Jesuit.

POEM 88
Translated by Rosanna Warren

According to Marthe Bibesco's *Au Bal avec Marcel Proust*, Proust first saw her at the Salle Pleyel and "found her superior to the Duchesse de Hugo." Princess Marthe Bibesco (1886–1951), a cousin of Antoine Bibesco, was born Princess Marta Lothari of Romania. She was author, most famously, of *Les Huit Paradis* (The Eight Paradises) and *Alexandre Asiatique* (Alexander in Asia).

The entire poem is reproduced in *Au Bal avec Marcel Proust*. In the English version, *Marcel Proust at the Ball*, Bibesco notes that it cannot be translated because of the intricacy of the rhymes. The addressee of the poem, Emmanuel Bibesco, committed suicide on August 22, 1917, according to friends, after a long and painful illness, though others have intimated that he did so because he could not come to terms with his homosexuality. For an appreciation of Emmanuel Bibesco, see *Enid Bagnold's Autobiography* and her play *The Last Joke*. For Proust's appreciation of Emmanuel Bibesco, see his letter to Antoine Bibesco (dated!) August 27, 1917, and published in the journal *La Destra: Rivista internazionale di cultura et politica* in December 1971.

Line 5   Nohant is a commune in central France where George Sand (née Amantine Lucile Aurore Dupin, later Baroness Dudevant, 1804–1876) spent part of her childhood and adult life (some of it in the company of Frederic Chopin; they also spent time together on the island of Mallorca), doing much of her writing in the house originally owned by her grandmother. Her novel *François le champi* is an important referent in RTP. Henri Amic was a young writer who befriended George Sand, spending time with her in Nohant.

Line 8   Proust used the car-hire company Unic Motorcars for transportation throughout Normandy. He later established a liaison with one of its drivers, Alfred Agostinelli.

Line 9   Pornic is a small town on the Atlantic coast in southeastern Brittany, about twenty miles from Nantes. Balzac was one of the writers who used to visit there.

Line 18   Stourdza is a Romanian noble family.

Line 20   Proust first saw Marthe Bibesco from afar at a performance of Wagner's *Tristan and Isolde*, in which the lead was sung by tenor Ernest van Dyck.

Lines 22 and 23   Eustaziu, Popesco, Nicolaïde, and Grescesco are traditional Romanian family names.

Poems 89 to 92

Along with Antoine Bibesco, Bertrand de Salignac-Fénelon (1878–1914) was part of Proust's inner circle. He met Proust in 1901 and they traveled together to the Low Countries to look at art (see introduction to "Portraits de peintres").

POEM 89
Translated by Charlotte Mandell

Line 1   Most likely refers to Enguerrand I (1042–1106) who divorced his first wife and then married his second when she was still married to someone else.

Line 2   The Golden Fleece and Medea's skill refers to the Greek myth. In addition to the myth, Proust would have been familiar with Corneille's play *Médée* (1635).

Line 5   Antoine Bibesco. See notes to poems 84 and 87. Bibesco introduced Proust to Fénelon.

Line 6   René Blum, younger brother of writer and politician Léon Blum, who helped negotiate the publication of *Swann's Way*. See notes to Poem 47.

Line 9   For information on Henry de Jouvenel, see notes
          to Poem 47. For information on Reynaldo Hahn,
          see notes to "Poèmes à/Poems to" before Poem 55.

Line 10   The translator playfully changes *le lévite* (most
          likely reference to a Jewish tailor and/or a type of
          overcoat) to Rogers Peet, an American menswear
          brand founded in 1874 and well known in the
          mid-twentieth century in the United States.

Poems 90 and 91: Two Verse Notes on Hospitality

Perhaps Proust's most famous letter to his cook was sent to
Céline Cottin, in which he wrote to thank her for a beef in aspic
she had made for his birthday celebration in 1907, and which
included the line, "Would that my prose were as solid as your
aspic." The beef in aspic would appear in RTP.

POEM 90
Translated by Meena Alexander

For more information on Fénelon, see the introduction to "Portraits de peintres" and the notes to poems 47 and 86.

POEM 91
Translated by Susan Stewart

For more information on Fénelon, see the introduction to "Portraits de peintres" and the notes to poems 47 and 86. Note for line 2: It's possible that Proust was referring to rosé wine, which would have paired well with cold roast chicken, but left off the accent.

POEM 92
Translated by Charlotte Mandell

Line 4   Bertrand de Salignac-Fénelon.

POEM 93
Translated by Jennifer Moxley

The Marquis Louis d'Albufera (1877–1953) was a good friend of Proust's and a model for Robert de St. Loup in RTP. Roger Shattuck called him "an unbookish rake." For several years his mistress was the young Louisa de Mornand; Proust acted as a go-between when they were at odds and particularly when Albufera announced his engagement. See Poem 83 and its note.

In 1908 Proust wrote to Albufera that he was working on something that was:

A study on the nobility
A Parisian novel
An essay on Saint-Beuve and Flaubert
An essay on women
An essay on pederasty (not easy to publish)
A study of stained-glass windows
A study on tombstones
A study on the novel

A well-known story of Proust's relationship with Albufera, which Proust reported to Antoine Bibesco, concerned a telephone conversation between the two of them in 1914, regarding *Swann's Way*:

"But, my dear Louis, have you read my book?" "Read your book? You've written a book?" "Of course, Louis; I've even sent you a copy." "Well, my little Marcel, if you sent it to me, I must certainly have read it. The only trouble is that I wasn't quite sure that I had ever had it."

Line 26   Among Proust and his friends, "tombeau" was code for a secret.

Line 42   Proust and his circle often dined at restaurant Larue in the place de la Madeleine, at the corner of rue Royale.

POEM 94
Translated by Mark Polizzotti

The Comte Greffulhe (1848–1932) was a model for the duc de Guermantes. He was fabulously wealthy and married to one of the great beauties of the time (see note to Poem 95 below) and had a reputation as a domestic tyrant.

Line 1   Bois-Boudran was Greffulhe's estate near Melun, Seine-et-Marne, about forty miles southeast of Paris.

POEM 95
Translated by Charlotte Mandell

The Comtesse Greffulhe (1860–1952) was born Élisabeth de Caraman-Chimay, the daughter of Prince Joseph de Chimay (1836–1892) and Marie de Montesquiou-Fézensac (1834–1884). Along with the Comtesse de Chevigné, she became one of Proust's fascinations and a model for the duchesse de Guermantes in RTP. She was beautiful, elegant, sophisticated, and extraordinarily self-centered. At the age of eighteen, her fortune diminished by family expenditure, she married the recently ennobled but fabulously wealthy Comte Henri Greffulhe (see notes to Poem 94). Proust saw her for the first time in 1893 at the home of Mme de Wagram. The Comtesse Élisabeth Greffulhe was painted by Philip de László, Paul César Helleu (1859–1927), and Antonio de La Gandara (1861–1917). She was a cousin of the poet Robert de Montesquiou (Fézensac) on her mother's side, to whom she once wrote, "I have never been understood save by you and the sun."

Comtesse Greffulhe lived at 10, rue d'Astorg, where her salons gathered the prominent from artistic and social circles. In her book *Other People's Letters*, Mina Curtiss relates how in 1948 Élisabeth de Clermont-Tonnerre (see notes to Poem 98) arranged a visit to rue d'Astorg, telling her that the comtesse wanted her to write a biography of Montesquiou, whom Curtiss loathed (by reading and reputation). During the visit the comtesse related that she did not like Proust. Comtesse Greffulhe died in 1952.

Élisabeth Greffulhe has been called one of the most important patrons of music at the turn of the last century (along with the duc and duchesse de Polignac). She introduced Gabriel Fauré to the world and helped bring the Ballets Russes to France (one of Proust's last social appearances was at the Hotel Majestic in 1922, where he went to celebrate the first public performance of Stravinsky's ballet *Le Renard* with Sergei Diaghilev, Vaslav Nijinsky, and Pablo Picasso, by the Ballets Russes).

The Comtesse Greffulhe's daughter Elaine married Proust's close friend the duc de Guiche, later the duc de Gramont, and she became the duchesse de Gramont (see poems 98 and 99).

Line 2   For information on Gaston Arman de Caillavet, see notes to Poem 8.

Line 10   Most likely Comte Louis de Turenne, a close friend of the Comtesse Greffulhe.

Abel Hermant (1861–1950) was a prolific poet, dramatist, and novelist.

POEM 96
Translated by Jeff Clark

Lines 8
and 11
Paul Verlaine (1844–1896), French poet

Line 13
Maman Colibri was a play by Henry Bataille (1872–1922); it premiered in 1904 and was reprised in 1911.

Line 18
Roger Puylagarde was an actor who played in the 1911 production of *Maman Colibri.*

Line 19
Painter Jean-Louis Forain (1852–1932) was a good friend of Proust's. If the caricature by SEM (Georges Goursat) is any guide, his face looked as if it were made of slightly melted wax. Influenced by his close friends Edgar Degas and Honoré Daumier, Forain was also a caricaturist; his work appeared in *Le Figaro* (to which Proust also contributed) and in the official salons of the time. Like Degas, he was an anti-Dreyfusard. According to Philippe Jullian, he was a great wit.

Line 21
Dr. Henri Cazalis (1840–1909), who wrote symbolist poetry under the pseudonyms of Jean Caselli and Jean Lahor, was a friend of Proust's father.

Line 22
Roger Monteaux (1879–1974) acted in the first production of *Maman Colibri.*

Lines 22
and 23
Francis and Gontier quote Cocteau in the *Bulletin Marcel Proust,* no. 13, 1963 (in which this poem first appeared), as writing, "This must be Kem or Ken, cheese á la Kem. I've forgotten who Marcel was talking about."

POEM 97

Translated by Jeff Clark

For information on Nijinsky, see notes to Poem 51. For information on Larue, see notes to Poem 90.

Line 10   *Indiana* was a popular song of the time.

POEM 98

Translated by Charlotte Mandell

Kolb notes that this poem was probably written "around April 17, 1906." According to Marthe Bibesco's book *The Veiled Wanderer,* the poem was a dedication to the duc de Guiche (1879–1962) inscribed on the flyleaf of a copy of *Les Plaisirs et les jours.* Guiche was the son of Agénor, duc de Gramont, and his second wife, Marguerite de Rothschild (1855–1905). By his first wife, Isabelle de Beauvau, the elder duc de Gramont had fathered Élisabeth de Gramont, later Elisabeth de Clermont-Tonnerre (1875–1954) who wrote two books on Proust (they were good friends), among other works, including a translation of the poetry of John Keats. She has also come down to history as a lover of American writer Natalie Barney.

Marthe Bibesco noted that "this Guiche is as handsome as a young David: pale complexion and violet-eyed, tall and of good carriage, the easy bearing of a man accustomed to physical exertion." Where Guiche and Proust met is unsettled—Marthe Bibesco says their meeting took place at the home of Geneviève Strauss but Proust biographer Jean-Yves Tadié suggests it was at the home of poet Anna de Noailles. Most likely, Proust had already met Guiche's parents at the salon of the aging Princesse Mathilde. In 1904, Proust's Gramont married Elaine Greffulhe, daughter of Élisabeth, Comtesse Greffulhe (1860–1952), who was one of the models for the Comtesse de Guermantes in RTP (see notes to poems 94 and 95).

Line 3   Garcia-Sanche, Duke of Larboust, was the founder of the House of Gramont.

Line 5   Armand d'Aure is the family name of the House of Gramont. See note above.

Line 8   The dedicatee of this poem was actually the *twelfth* duc de Guiche.

          Note: the de Guiche/Gramont family, depicted in an earlier era, appears prominently in *Cyrano de Bergerac* by Edmond de Rostand (1868–1917), which was first produced in 1896.

POEM 99

Translated by Charlotte Mandell

See notes to Poem 98 for information on Armand de Gramont, the duc de Guiche.

Line 1   Harry Relph, known as Little Tich [*sic*], was a British music-hall clown famous for his various characters. He was only four feet, six inches tall.

POEM 100

Translated by Mark Polizzotti

The person closest to Proust in the last years of his life was his housekeeper, Céleste Albaret (née Augustine Célestine Gineste, 1891–1984). She was born and raised in Auxillac and went to live in Proust's home in 1913 after her marriage to Proust's driver, Odilon Albaret, where she supplanted the busybody housekeeper and cook Céline Cottin (see notes to Poem 40). For the next nine years she subordinated her life to his. According to all accounts, even her speech patterns began to approximate his, a style reflected in her 1974 biography/autobiography *Monsieur Proust*, which was made into Percy Adlon's 1980 film *Céleste*. After Proust's death, Céleste and Odilon bought a small, run-down hotel in the rue des Canettes in Paris's sixth arrondissement. Later she became the caretaker of the Musée Ravel in Montfort l'Amaury.

Céleste's name appears in RTP, along with that of her sister, when two energetic young women visit the narrator in his hotel room in Balbec.

Line 7   Albert Nègre was the archbishop of Tours and the uncle of Céleste's second brother's wife. Céleste had four brothers, descriptive portraits of whom appear in her memoir.

POEM 101
Translated by Jeff Clark

This poem is a parody of Proust's own work "Paulus Potter" (poem 19 in this collection).

Line 5   Proust's housekeeper, Céleste Albaret, was born and raised in Auxillac, a small town about seventy-five miles south of Clermont-Ferrand. See notes to Poem 100.

Line 7   La Canourgue is a small town in the south of France, near Auxillac. It is often called Little Venice for the canals that run through it. Céleste Albaret's husband, Odilon, went to school there.

Line 9   François-Regis Gineste (?–1904) was the older brother of Proust's housekeeper Céleste Albaret (née Gineste).

POEM 102

Translated by Anna Moschovakis

Proust's poem was written as a response to Paul Morand's "Ode to Marcel Proust," published in the collection *Lampes à Arc* (1919):

OMBRE

Née de la fumée de vos fumigations,[1]
Le visage et la voix
Mangés
Par l'usage de la nuit
Céleste,[2]
Avec sa vigueur, douce, me trempe dans le jus noir
De votre chambre
Qui sent le bouchon tiède et la cheminée morte.

Derrière l'écran des cahiers,
Sous la lampe blonde et poisseuse comme une confiture,
Votre visage gît sous un traversin de craie.
Vous me tendez des mains gantées de filoselle ;[3]
Silencieusement votre barbe repousse
Au fond de vos joues.
Je dis :
—vous avez l'air d'aller fort bien.
Vous répondez :
—Cher ami, j'ai failli mourir trois fois dans la journée.
Vos fenêtres à tout jamais fermées
Vous refusent au boulevard Haussmann
Rempli à pleins bords,
Comme une auge brillante,

Du fracas de tôle des tramways.
Peut-être n'avez-vous jamais vu le soleil ?
Mais vous l'avez reconstitué, comme Lemoine, si véridique,
Que vos arbres fruitiers dans la nuit
Ont donné les fleurs.

Votre nuit n'est pas notre nuit :
C'est plein des lueurs blanches
Des catleyas[4] et des robes d'Odette,
Cristaux des flûtes, des lustres
Et des jabots tuyautés du général de Froberville.
Votre voix, blanche[5] aussi, trace une phrase si longue
Qu'on dirait qu'elle plie, alors que comme un malade
Sommeillant qui se plaint,
Vous dites : qu'on vous a fait un énorme chagrin.

Proust, à quels raouts[6] allez-vous donc la nuit
Pour en revenir avec des yeux si las et si lucides ?
Quelles frayeurs à nous interdites avez-vous connues
Pour en revenir si indulgent et si bon ?
Et sachant les travaux des âmes
Et ce qui se passe dans les maisons,
Et que l'amour fait si mal ?

Étaient-ce de si terribles veilles que vous y laissâtes
Cette rose fraicheur
Du portrait de Jacques-Émile Blanche ?
Et que vous voici, ce soir,
Pétri de la pâleur docile des cires
Mais heureux que l'on croie à votre agonie douce
De dandy gris perle et noir ?

SHADE

Born of the fumes of your fumigations
Face and voice
Devoured
By nocturnal use
Céleste,
Gently for all her harshness steeps me in the fluid darkness
Of your room
Redolent of fresh-pulled corks and dying embers
Behind the screen of manuscript
Under the pale lamp that is sticky with jam
Your face lies on a chalk-white bolster
You hold forth your hands gloved in silken floss
Silently your beard grows out
To the edges of your cheeks.

I say
"You seem to be doing pretty well."
You answer:
"My friend, I almost died three times today."
Your windows forever closed
Withhold you from the Boulevard Haussmann
Filled to the side walls
With the metal clangor of trams
Perhaps you have never seen the sun.
But, like Lemoine, you have reconstructed
So well
That in the night your fruit-trees
Have yielded blossoms.
Your night is not our night.

It is full of white gleamings
Of rare orchids and of Odette's gowns
Of champagne glasses and chandeliers
And the frilled shirt-fronts of General Froberville.

Your voice, white, too, winds through so long a sentence
It seems to fold, when like a patient
Complaining in his sleep
You say they've brought you a tremendous sorrow.

Proust, to what revels do you go by night
That you return with eyes so worn, so lucid?
What frights beyond our scope have come to you
That you are so indulgent and so kind?
And so aware of the travail of soul
And of what passes within dwellings
And that love brings ill?

Where they dread vigils that have left in you
The rosy bloom
Of the Jacques-Emile Blanche portrait?—
You here, tonight,
Steeped in the yielding pallor of the tapers
But happy that we believe in your calm agony
Of black and pearl-grey dandy?

PAUL MORAND, 1915

Notes [by Paul Morand]

1. A treatment that consisted of exposing a part of
    the body to medicinal fumes or vapors
2. Céleste Albaret, Marcel Proust's housekeeper

3. Uneven thread that comes from a silk pod
4. Tropical American plant cultivated for its beautiful flowers [editor's note: in RTP, the catleyas is the name of the flower Odette and Swann used as a code for embarking on sex.]
5. Certainly like lights but also like Proust's nights and like the collection *Blanche* (White) from the publishers Gallimard
6. Meeting, society party

Editor's note: This translation is reprinted from Joseph T. Shipley, *Modern French Poetry* (New York: Greenberg, 1926). I assume it is Shipley's translation.

Paul Morand (1888–1976) was a writer and diplomat who was introduced to Proust by their mutual friend Henri Bardac; he was married to Proust's good friend, the Princesse Soutzo. Proust provided the introduction to Morand's book *Tendres Stock* (translated as *Fancy Goods*), which is often considered one of Proust's important statements of theory and thought on literature. Despite the ill feelings engendered by Morand's poem, they were soon reconciled and after Proust's death Morand became the president of the Société des Amis de Marcel Proust (the dedication in Ramon Fernández's 1943 book *À la Gloire de Proust* reads: "To Paul Morand, To the president of the Marcel Proust Society, to the astute painter of our era, who knows what it owes to he who one day went off in search of lost time in order to give us the gift of revelations about time regained"). A good appreciation of the Proust-Morand relationship appeared in the *Bulletin des Amis de Marcel Proust et des Amis de Combray*, no. 27, 1977. One side note: in 1928, at a fancy ball at the home of Baba and Jean-Louis de Faucigny-Lucinge focused on fashions of the period 1880 to 1905, for which many invitees dressed as characters from RTP, Morand went as the Baron de Charlus.

POEM 103

Translated by Harold Augenbraum

Written on a single, small sheet of paper without erasures. It seems to have been a quickly scrawled note to Céleste Albaret. Not included in the 1982 journal publication, it came to light when it was sold at auction at Christie's in London.

POEM 104

Translated by Harold Augenbraum

Written on school paper, most likely when Proust and Boissonnas attended the École Libre des sciences-politiques together in early 1892, along with Robert de Billy.

This poem was published in the *Bulletin de la Société des Amis de Marcel Proust et de Combray,* no. 27, 1977, but not included in the 1982 compilation by Francis and Gontier. See note to Poem 46 for more information on Jean Boissonnas.

About the Translators

Meena Alexander has published many volumes of poetry, including *Illiterate Heart* (winner of the PEN Open Book Award), *Raw Silk,* and *Quickly Changing River.* She has received awards from the John Simon Guggenheim Foundation, Fulbright Foundation, Rockefeller Foundation for a residency at Bellagio, and the Arts Council of England. She is Distinguished Professor of English at CUNY Graduate Center and Hunter College.

Mary Ann Caws is Distinguished Professor of English, French, and Comparative Literature at the Graduate Center of the City University of New York, author of many volumes on art and text, and most recently of *Surprised in Translation, Salvador Dalí,* and *Provençal Cooking: Savoring the Simple Life in France.*

Nicholas Christopher is the author of eight volumes of poetry, most recently, *Crossing the Equator: New & Selected Poems;* six novels, including *Tiger Rag,* published by the Dial Press in 2013, and *A Trip to the Stars;* and a book about film noir, *Somewhere in the Night.* He is a professor in the School of the Arts at Columbia University. Anna Oancea, his translating partner for these poems, is a doctoral candidate in the Department of French & Romance Philology at Columbia University. Her dissertation examines the representation of inventors in late nineteenth-century literature.

Jeff Clark is a typographer who lives in Ypsilanti, Michigan.

Lydia Davis's works include a novel, *The End of the Story,* and four full-length story collections—*Varieties of Disturbance* (2007), *Samuel Johnson Is Indignant* (2002), *Almost No Memory* (1997), and *Break It Down* (1986). She translated Gustave Flaubert's *Madame Bovary* and Marcel Proust's *Swann's Way* for Penguin Classics.

Marcella Durand's books include *Deep Eco Pré* (with Tina Darragh, Little Red Leaves, 2009); *AREA* (Belladonna Books, 2008); and *Traffic & Weather*, a site-specific poem written during a residency at the Lower Manhattan Cultural Council (Futurepoem Books, 2008). Her translating partner and father, Michel Durand, is a retired painter and master printer.

Richard Howard is the author of numerous volumes of poetry, including *Without Saying*, which was a finalist for the National Book Award; *Inner Voices*; *Trappings: New Poems*; *Like Most Revelations: New Poems*; *Selected Poems*; *No Traveler*; *Untitled Subjects*, for which he received the Pulitzer Prize; and *Quantities*. He has published more than 150 translations from the French, including works by Gide, Giraudoux, Cocteau, Camus, De Beauvoir, De Gaulle, Breton, Robbe-Grillet, Barthes, Cioran, Claude Simon, Stendhal, and Baudelaire's *Les Fleurs du mal*.

Wayne Koestenbaum has published fifteen books of poetry, criticism, and fiction, including *Humiliation*, *The Anatomy of Harpo Marx*, *Blue Stranger with Mosaic Background*, *Hotel Theory*, *Best-Selling Jewish Porn Films*, and *Moira Orfei in Aigues-Mortes*. He is a Distinguished Professor of English at the CUNY Graduate Center.

Charlotte Mandell is a literary translator who lives in the Hudson Valley with her husband, the poet Robert Kelly. She has translated over thirty books, including works by Blanchot, Proust (*The Lemoine Affair*, a collection of his pastiches), Flaubert, and Jean-Luc Nancy. Her most recent translated novels are Jonathan Littell's *The Kindly Ones* and Mathias Énard's *Zone*, a 517-page sentence.

Wyatt Mason is a contributing writer for the *New York Times Magazine*, a contributing editor for *Harper's*, and editor at large for the Margellos World Republic of Letters series at Yale University Press. His writing appears in *GQ*, *The New Yorker*, and the *New York Review of Books*, and his translations of the complete works of Arthur Rimbaud are published by Modern Library.

Anna Moschovakis is the translator of *The Jokers* by Albert Cossery, nominated for a Best Translated Book Award and a French-American Foundation translation prize. Also a poet, she is an editor at Ugly Duckling Presse and a core faculty member of Bard College's Milton Avery Graduate School of the Arts.

Jennifer Moxley is the author of five books of poetry, a memoir, and a book of essays. She has translated books by contemporary French poets Anne Portugal and Jacqueline Risset. She is a professor of poetry and poetics at the University of Maine.

Mark Polizzotti's books include *Revolution of the Mind: The Life of André Breton*, a monograph on Luis Buñuel's *Los Olvidados*, and *Bob Dylan's Highway 61 Revisited*. The translator of over forty books from the French, he heads the publications program at The Metropolitan Museum of Art in New York.

Susan Stewart is a poet, critic, and translator. Her most recent books of poems are *Red Rover* and *Columbarium*, which won the National Book Critics Circle Award for poetry. Among her many prose works are *The Poet's Freedom* and *Poetry and the Fate of the Senses*. She is a former MacArthur Fellow and the Avalon Foundation University Professor in the Humanities at Princeton University.

Cole Swensen is the author of fourteen books of poetry; the most recent is *Gravesend*. She has translated some fifteen volumes of works by contemporary French writers. She is the founding editor of the small press La Presse and teaches at Brown University.

Deborah Treisman is the fiction editor of *The New Yorker* and a Chevalier of the Ordre des Arts et des Lettres. Her translations have appeared in *The New Yorker*, *The Nation*, *Harper's*, and *Grand Street* and she is the editor of the anthology *20 Under 40: Stories from The New Yorker*.

Rosanna Warren teaches at the University of Chicago. Her book of criticism, *Fables of the Self: Studies in Lyric Poetry*, came out in 2008. Her most recent book of poems is *Ghost in a Red Hat* (2011). She has received awards from the Academy of American Poets, The American Academy of Arts & Letters, and the Lila Wallace Foundation, among others.

Lauren Watel received the 2012 Mississippi Review Prize in fiction. Her fiction, poetry, and translations have appeared in *Ploughshares*, *TriQuarterly*, *Five Points*, *Mississippi Review*, *Poetry International*, and *Slate*.

THE STORY OF PENGUIN CLASSICS

Before 1946 . . . "Classics" are mainly the domain of academics and students; readable editions for everyone else are almost unheard of. This all changes when a little-known classicist, E. V. Rieu, presents Penguin founder Allen Lane with the translation of Homer's *Odyssey* that he has been working on in his spare time.

1946 Penguin Classics debuts with *The Odyssey*, which promptly sells three million copies. Suddenly, classics are no longer for the privileged few.

1950s Rieu, now series editor, turns to professional writers for the best modern, readable translations, including Dorothy L. Sayers's *Inferno* and Robert Graves's unexpurgated *Twelve Caesars*.

1960s The Classics are given the distinctive black covers that have remained a constant throughout the life of the series. Rieu retires in 1964, hailing the Penguin Classics list as "the greatest educative force of the twentieth century."

1970s A new generation of translators swells the Penguin Classics ranks, introducing readers of English to classics of world literature from more than twenty languages. The list grows to encompass more history, philosophy, science, religion, and politics.

1980s The Penguin American Library launches with titles such as *Uncle Tom's Cabin* and joins forces with Penguin Classics to provide the most comprehensive library of world literature available from any paperback publisher.

1990s The launch of Penguin Audiobooks brings the classics to a listening audience for the first time, and in 1999 the worldwide launch of the Penguin Classics Web site extends their reach to the global online community.

The 21st Century Penguin Classics are completely redesigned for the first time in nearly twenty years. This world-famous series now consists of more than 1,300 titles, making the widest range of the best books ever written available to millions—and constantly redefining what makes a "classic."

The Odyssey continues . . .

The best books ever written

PENGUIN 🐧 CLASSICS

SINCE 1946

Find out more at www.penguinclassics.com

CLICK ON A CLASSIC
www.penguinclassics.com

The world's greatest literature at your fingertips

Constantly updated information on more than a thousand titles,
from Icelandic sagas to ancient Indian epics, Russian drama to
Italian romance, American greats to African masterpieces

•

The latest news on recent additions to the list, updated
editions, and specially commissioned translations

•

Original essays by leading writers

•

A wealth of background material, including biographies
of every classic author from Aristotle to Zamyatin, plot
synopses, readers' and teachers' guides, useful Web links

•

Online desk and examination copy assistance for academics

•

Trivia quizzes, competitions, giveaways, news on
forthcoming screen adaptations